Christen Købke

CHRISTEN KØBKE

Sanford Schwartz

t Timken Publishers

LIBRARY OF CONGRESS CATALOGING-IN-PUBLICATION DATA

Schwartz, Sanford.
    Christen Købke / Sanford Schwartz.
        p.   cm.
    Includes bibliographical references and index.
    ISBN 0-943221-15-3 : $35.00
     1. Købke, Christen. 1810–1848 — Criticism and interpretation.   I. Title.
    ND723.K6S38   1992
    759.89 — dc20   92-20771
                                 CIP

Type set in Janson Text by Wilsted and Taylor
Designed by David Bullen
Printed by Stamperia Valdonega, Verona, Italy

Frontispiece: *Portion of the Plaster Cast Collection at Charlottenborg*, 1830. Oil on canvas, 16 3/8 × 14 1/8″ (42 × 35.5 cm). Hirschsprungske Samling, Copenhagen

CONTENTS

One of the Turrets at Frederiksborg Castle,
1831(?). Black and brown ink, gray wash,
9⅞ × 7⅛" (25.2 × 18.2 cm). Kongelige
Kobberstiksamling, Statens Museum for
Kunst, Copenhagen.

Acknowledgments

I want to thank Steingrim Laursen for telling me, from the first, that this book could be done. I am grateful to many people in Denmark: Elsemarie Gade, Marianne Saabye, Dan A. Marmorstein, Anneli Fuchs, Flemming Johansen, Claus M. Smidt, Tine Seligmann, Dorthe Aagesen, Kjeld von Folsach, Anne Lise Thygesen, Marianne Ertberg, Vilads Viladsen, Leis Iversen, Liss and Tyge Brandt, Vibeke Weiersøe, Vibeke Knudsen, Berthe Bülow, Lennart Gottlieb, Helle Lassen, Jytte Harboe, Helle Pade, Kristian Jacobsen, Hanne Nielsen, Bodil Sander, Finn T. Frederiksen, and Emma Salling. It was a rare experience to have worked with so many unassuming, forthright, and encouraging individuals. I am indebted to Kasper Monrad for his careful critical reading of the manuscript. If any misstatements remain, they are my own. And I appreciate the kind consideration of Matthias Wohlgemuth. On this side of the Atlantic, I'd like to thank Robert Rosenblum, who also urged me on, and Jane Timken, who wanted to do *Christen Købke*. I am thankful to Anna Jardine and Reid Sherline for making my manuscript a much better piece of writing. My special thanks are for Joshua Kirsch.

This book is for Carole Obedin, with love and admiration.

Self-Portrait, 1833. Oil on canvas,
16½ × 14″ (42 × 35.5 cm). Statens Museum
for Kunst, Copenhagen.

Introduction

Like images seen through a telescope, Christen Købke's pictures have the quality of having just come into focus, as if in the next second they'll become blurry again. There is a particular glinting, lightweight clarity to this early-nineteenth-century Danish painter's realism. The surfaces of his paintings are even and rarely luscious—though they aren't dry. And the light his pictures give off is soft and gentle, almost fuzzy with whitish particles. Looking at Købke's portraits and his scenes of everyday life on a perpetual summer's day in the environs of Copenhagen, we're made keenly conscious of the edges of shapes. Razor-sharp lines of light appear to stream forth from where, say, in a portrait, the outline of the sitter's shape touches the background. We seem to see the pre-industrial world through the eyes of an artist who is somehow acquainted with a mechanized way of seeing. It's as if, going through the history of art, no artist before Købke had presented the world with quite this degree of light in the air.

Christen Købke (pronounced keub-kuh) lived from 1810 to 1848, and most of his work is from a roughly eight-year period in the 1830s. He is sometimes written about by Danes as their finest painter ever, yet he's virtually unknown beyond Scandinavia—beyond Denmark, really—and it isn't a surprise that he has been overlooked. His body of work is relatively small, and his pictures are generally quite small, too. They're also quiet and intimate in tone.

Købke painted primarily portraits and what might be called landscape views. They're informally direct pictures of lanes and walks, or of the sky from a rooftop, or of historical sites. Often there will be a glimpse of a pond or a bay nearby, with people, buildings, ships' masts, or a chimney in the foreground or in the far distance. To hear them described, his pictures might seem like old postcards of the sleepy doings of some village in rural Wisconsin.

There's nothing antiquarian, though, about an actual Købke painting. The pleasure of his work is physical and immediate. The small size of his pictures, and his hairbreadth realism—the number of details he packs into paintings that can be ten inches or less on a side—make him virtually a miniaturist. Yet this superfine realism doesn't seem fussy or painstaking; we're not made conscious of a particular artist who is showing off. We're simply transported to the scene. After the second it takes for our eyes to adjust to Købke's images, his pictures don't even seem particularly small.

And many of the people in his portraits, which are also quite small, have the force and roundedness of certain characters in nineteenth-century literature. After seeing Købke's portrait of a somewhat rickety yet radiant and self-possessed old woman named Johanne Pløyen (pl. 37), to take one example, we can go away thinking that Johanne Pløyen is someone we have known—maybe one of the best people we've known.

How obscure is Købke? It's probably fair to say that, certainly in the United States and perhaps everywhere outside northern Europe, he is a name for no more than a small circle of scholars, museum curators, and connoisseurs of the period. Over the years, he has been referred to only in wide-ranging histories of nineteenth-century painting, such as Fritz Novotny's *Painting and Sculpture in Europe 1780–1880* (1960), which includes many acute observations on him. Robert Rosenblum's affectionate and insightful paragraphs on Købke, in his influential survey *19th-Century Art* (1984), may be the most extensive writing on the artist by an American.

Købke's pictures have rarely been seen outside Denmark, either. His entire history of exhibitions beyond Scandinavia amounts to very little. Besides being a part of an exhibition of Danish nineteenth-century painting in Paris in 1928, and of one in Kiel, (then West) Germany, in 1968, he was included in, among a few others, the Royal Academy's Neoclassicism exhibition in London in 1972 and the Museum of Modern Art's *Before Photography* in New York in 1981. He wasn't, of course, featured in any of these shows.

It wasn't until 1984 and 1985, with an exhibition of early-nineteenth-century Danish painting held at the National Gallery in London, and then (in a somewhat different form) at the Grand Palais in Paris, that Købke was seen by a wider European public. The show opened eyes, at least, in the right places, because since then individual paintings by him have been bought by the National Gallery, London, and the National Gallery of Scotland, Edinburgh, and by four American museums: the J. Paul Getty Museum, in Malibu; the Cleveland Museum of Art; the Los Angeles County Museum of Art; and the Metropolitan Museum of Art, in New York. The latter two museums are currently planning a joint show of Danish art from Købke's period for 1993 and 1994.

My own discovery of Købke came when, looking at Geraldine Norman's *Biedermeier Painting* (1986) for information about another artist, I saw a large reproduction of his portrait of Frederik Sødring (pl. 15). The picture, which shows a young red-haired painter sitting casually in his studio, presenting the most open and friendly expression, had a striking formal elegance and warmth of feeling. Biedermeier art was produced mostly in German-speaking and Scandinavian countries from around 1815, after Napoleon's defeat at Waterloo and the quieting of Europe, to the late 1840s, when the political and social landscape became uncertain and volatile again everywhere. The Biedermeier world got its name from a character in a newspaper column—Gottlieb Biedermaier—invented in the middle of the nineteenth century to poke fun at the period just over. Bumbling, timorous, and pedantic, Gottlieb Biedermaier was seen as the essence of an era in retreat, or, at least, stagnation. It was also an era that placed a new value on domesticity and that, as art historians have increasingly shown, saw a quiet revolution in the arts and articles of daily life: architecture, furniture, clothing, utensils. Købke's *The Landscape Painter F. Sødring*, which exudes a sunny contentment with the here and now, was certainly of this world. But Købke's painting had a big, full-bodied scale, and the sitter himself a presence, that made me forget Biedermeier art.

And when I eventually saw Købke in Denmark—the bulk of his work can be found in a number of museums in Copenhagen—I found, if not an imposing figure or an innovator, then a painter whose finest pictures bear comparison with the masterworks of many eras. Købke's endeavor is remarkably lean and optical, and it's without sentiment. His art in one way is about nothing more than sheer looking; he's an analyst of the space within a painting. He speaks the language of some Italian Early Renaissance painters and some Dutch seventeenth-century Little Masters; of relatively isolated figures, such as Canaletto, and of the more intellectual painters of late-nineteenth-century France, such as Degas and Seurat. Like these (and numerous twentieth-century) artists, Købke excites us, in part, for his witty, dreamy, and poetic play on nearness and farness in a picture, and on what our, the audience's, distance is from the image. The particular degree of his miniaturist's realism, as it relates to the various sizes of his pictures, is what makes his work pulse.

Købke painted during a moment known loosely in Denmark as the

Golden Age. The term was originally a literary designation, but it has come to refer to Danish life and culture in general at the time— roughly the first half of the 1800s. There was undeniably a blooming of talent in many fields: the sciences, the plastic arts, poetry and the novel, the theater and ballet, theology, philosophy. Søren Kierke- gaard and Hans Christian Andersen were of this world, which was rather small and centered entirely in Copenhagen, the seat of the monarchy. The two writers could have attended the Royal Theater in Kongens Nytorv, where they might have seen the latest production of August Bournonville on the same night.

Also on Kongens Nytorv—literally, "king's new square"—was the Royal Academy of Fine Arts. It was housed in Charlottenborg Palace, and the Academy as a whole, with all its sections, has long been re- ferred to as Charlottenborg. (The scene remains largely the same to- day, though the theater was rebuilt later in the 1800s.) In the 1820s, un- der the aegis of C. W. Eckersberg, a painter and a particularly gifted teacher, and N. L. Høyen, an art historian, museum director, and critic with a missionary zeal, Charlottenborg buzzed with young painting students. Denmark had never seen so many talented artists in a single generation. There had been few significant painters at all in the country's history.

Many of these students of the twenties, while not powerhouses, cre- ated distinct voices for themselves. And at a glance Købke, who was not especially esteemed in his lifetime, may not stand out. When they were first venturing forth—it was a high moment for most—they all painted quite small pictures of very similar subjects. But it doesn't take long to see the erectness, precision, and gentleness in Købke's art, and its freshly felt formal tension, that put him in a different sphere from his contemporaries.

Købke's story is one of youthful talent and genius—and the diffi- culty of going on from it. By age twelve, in 1822, he was a student at

Charlottenborg, and by 1829, at nineteen, he was on his way to a mature style. The vast majority of the pictures that we still want to look at were made between 1830 and the spring of 1838.

In the summer of the latter year, having turned twenty-eight, and now married, Købke went to Italy. The trip was an inevitability. Nearly every Danish artist of the time went, or had a good reason for not going. As far as Købke's contemporaries are concerned, we feel that while their early paintings, done in Denmark, are their liveliest, they generally painted the same way before, during, and after their stay abroad. With Købke, however, the trip signaled a genuine break. He never regained his compelling original subjects, and he didn't go on to something of substance.

In his last ten years, back home in Denmark, he labored mightily on pictures set in a not quite real, and not quite imaginary, Italy. The public wasn't taken with them, and neither, it seems, was Købke. The fire wasn't there. He produced progressively fewer works as the 1840s wore on, and these pictures, which don't have the stamp or flavor of any particular artist, are rarely featured in Danish museums. He died a few months short of his thirty-eighth birthday, of pneumonia, leaving his wife and two children.

Perhaps the single most all-encompassing perception about Købke is a statement by Emil Hannover, his first biographer, who wrote that because Købke "became a painter while still a child," he "cultivated the ability to see at the expense of all other abilities." It ought to be said that in 1822 it wasn't unusual to be attending the Academy at age twelve. Studying at Charlottenborg then was like being an apprentice in a trade school. And Købke was hardly the only boy getting instruction who developed into a full-fledged artist while still in his teens. At the time, significant accomplishments by young people were the order of the day throughout Europe. Spurred by revolution, the person of Napoleon, the wars of liberation, and the rise of new national states, one talent after another came into bloom before his time and, very often, was dead not long after making his mark. Quite a few of Købke's contemporaries and near contemporaries, whether English poets or watercolorists, German playwrights, Austrian composers, Italian essayists, or Russian novelists—or fellow Danish painters—lived shorter lives than he did.

What is different about Købke, and what Hannover means, is that the painter's vision is synonymous with a boy's way of seeing and responding to the world. Hannover is saying that, in tone, Købke's work runs the range from being somewhat blank to being youthfully—charmingly—trustful to conveying a jet of pure, frank, penetrating awareness.

Certainly it's appropriate to talk about Købke as someone whose major energies were set in motion while he was still a child. Family life was Købke's arena. He came from a large and fairly well-to-do family—his father was a big-time baker—and he did most of his work when he was living under his parents' roof. He continued to live with his parents even after he married and became a father. When many of his finest pictures are put together, the result is in a sense a family album. The portraits are, in considerable number, of family and friends, and in his views, which often have people in them somewhere, we come to believe that we're looking at family members posing for the artist—that, as in Jacques-Henri Lartigue's boyhood photographs, the artwork was almost a communal effort.

Købke seems to have thought of painting as a mixture of sport and private reckoning—a fight with himself to prove his mettle. He gave a number of paintings as gifts. It was probably easier for him to make a painting with the idea that it would please a particular person than with the idea that it would be an object at a salon, seen by strangers, there to advance everyone's sense of "Christen Købke." His work began to show strain only when he realized that he had to become a public figure. It's generally noted that Købke was personally unadventurous, that most of his pictures are of places he lived in or near. It has been remarked that he could always be home for dinner after a day out sketching or painting.

Yet when we have absorbed his portraits and his many views of this or that bit of the greater Copenhagen scene, indoors and out, and when we've compared him with his contemporaries, we're primarily aware of how wide and inclusive Købke was. No other Danish painter of the time presents so many faces, views, and scenes of everyday life that we still want to look at. Købke might be telling the national story of Denmark, though what we're given is more a mood than a story.

Købke's way of painting nothing more than what an eye sees corresponds, so a non-Dane can believe, to a larger note in Danish life. It is a state of being attuned to the sheer momentariness of things. In this Købke resembles (again to an outsider) both Andersen and Kierkegaard. A storyteller/playwright/novelist and a philosopher/theologian/polemicist—they were both one-of-a-kind literary creators—can barely be compared with each other, let alone with a painter. But it's hard not to sense in Købke's pictures, if only for a moment, both Andersen's spirit and Kierkegaard's. Our setting is that of every once-upon-a-time kingdom, seen here on an ordinary yet budding, expectant day. And with the same passion that the narrator in *Fear and Trembling* seeks to pin down the meaning of faith, we feel that Købke works to make the most ordinary motif into an unbudgeably right image.

Købke was rediscovered by the Danes themselves in an exhibition in Copenhagen in 1884, where he was seen in depth in his native city for the first time in almost forty years (since an auction of his work held after his death). In 1893, Emil Hannover's pioneering, and wonderful, biography appeared, and in 1915, Mario Krohn, a museum director and a Købke family relative, published an illustrated catalogue of all the painter's known work at the time. Since then Købke has been written about in his homeland in various appreciations, small picture books, and art historical studies of phases of his art. A full, major biography by Hans Edvard Norregård-Nielsen, director of the Ny Carlsberg Foundation, is awaited, and Kasper Monrad, of the Statens Museum for Kunst, has laid out in a number of different publications an amazingly complete account of the lives and work of Købke and his contemporaries. Monrad is the primary author of *Danish Painting: The Golden Age*, the catalogue of the 1984 London show, an excellent guide that is also the only book in English on this particular period.

The biographical and critical appreciation that follows is not a work of scholarship; it builds on these and other writings. I see Købke's life and development in roughly the same way as do most Danish writers. About a few works, though, and about the importance of certain phases of his art, I have a considerably different opinion from what is generally expressed—and I hope I make it clear that my opinion is my own. Although my goal has been a critical and biographical introduction of Købke to an English-speaking audience, I've been propelled by the opportunity of seeing how he fits in relation to painters of his time who weren't Danish and to painters of all periods and nationalities. The comparisons I've drawn between Købke and Corot, or Watteau, or Piero della Francesca, or Canaletto, or any other painter, shouldn't be taken as my saying that Købke's art as a whole is the equal of this or that painter's art. Calling him, say, a Danish Watteau, I intend to create possible ways of looking at and thinking about Købke. It's hardly time to put him in a permanent niche.

If I've emphasized associations between Købke and the classic European painters it's also because, for all their care and perceptiveness, Danish writers about art generally brush by this topic. Købke's being unknown outside his homeland some hundred forty years after his death perhaps has to do as much with the Danish temperament as with the deceptively simple and undramatic nature of his work. Extremely modest and, beneath that, extremely patriotic, and, beneath both perhaps, dryly humorous, Danes seem to take it as a matter of course that things Danish probably aren't of interest to other people. Writing about Købke, I've felt as lucky, wary, and elated as a scout in unmapped territory. I have learned to appreciate what Jens Peter Jacobsen means when he says, of a character in one of his novels, that "he was fond of the slightly comical caution with which he had to express himself as soon as there was any mention of a comparison between Danish and foreign literature, or any time at all when Denmark was to be measured by something that wasn't Danish."

CHRISTEN KØBKE

POET OF THE SUBURBS

Although he's properly described as a man of a slightly different generation, Christen Købke's work years overlapped those of Corot and Constable and Caspar David Friedrich, and he shares qualities with each of them. They're all painters who look at the natural world as a source of strength and purity. And they all put major thoughts in small pictures.

Købke resembles Corot in that he wants to present the effects of an often diffused light and, also, unextraordinary moments. Like Corot, he's an orchestrator of closely related and overlapping tones; in a given painting each color feels weighted. When he sets a green wagon near a red fence, for instance, the surrounding colors are so balanced that the red and the green spring out on their own.

On occasion, though, Købke's colors are vivid, or odd, or capricious in a way that Corot's never are. The single-color backgrounds of some of Købke's portraits—a novel shade of green; an unexpected lavender—are often absorbing in themselves. A lake's water might be a pale grayish red and its little waves a dark plum red; a white sailboat, reflected in a lake at sunset, might be a tropical parrot green. There's also a sour red in his work; it's often used for bridges, and this (or a related) red can actually be found in Denmark today. Seeing it in use, one begins to believe that Købke's unpredictable and candy-like color

choices derived from what he actually saw—that he wasn't by temperament an expressionist or a formalist in his feeling for color (to borrow
another era's terms), but rather, someone who had the right combination of passivity and nerve to go where his eye led him. Købke
clearly knew an exquisite color when he saw it, but there isn't a single
painting where one feels him reaching for an effect.

Very much like Friedrich, and unlike Corot, Købke is a storyteller.
The Danish and the north German painter both set out to capture a
specific lyric instant; and there are a few Købke renderings of trees
with leafless branches that suggest a direct influence by the German
master.

Friedrich was some forty years older than Købke. He had studied at
the Royal Academy in Copenhagen in his early twenties (as had another eminent German Romantic painter, Philipp Otto Runge), and
he exhibited in Copenhagen in his later years. Købke and other Danish artists, then in their youthful prime, saw and responded to him. But
the Friedrich-like moments in Købke's work aren't more than moments. Købke's mood and sense of light, and his aims, are both more
down-to-earth and more perceptual and analytical than Friedrich's.
Købke, unlike the older painter, doesn't presume to paint made-up
scenes; he believes it's enough to paint what he sees directly before
him. There is a melancholy mood to Købke's pictures, but it arrives
from between the cracks.

Like Constable (and to some extent like Corot and Friedrich, although they're rarely thought about in this way), Købke paints what
might be called the suburban world. Dutch painters more or less invented the subject in the 1640s, and then it stopped mattering to European art for some two hundred years. The setting is a domain of for-
ests, fields, and bodies of water, yet it is also a site of country living, and

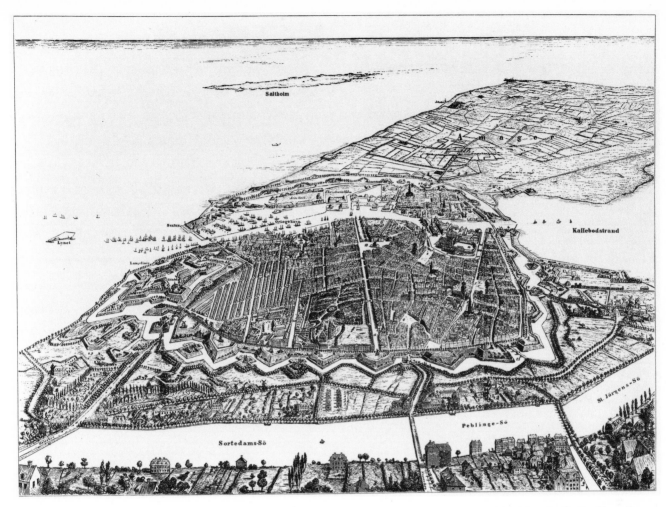

Conrad Seidelin, *Bird's-Eye View of Copenhagen*, 1856. Lithograph, 11¼ × 15⅝″ (28.7 × 39.6 cm). Kongelige Bibliotek, Copenhagen. Although made nearly twenty years after his death, this map gives a good sense of Købke's world. To the left, on the Sound, is the star-shaped Citadel. To the right, in the middle of the city, is an open space, the Kongens Nytorv, site of the Royal Academy of Fine Arts. In the lower left edge of the map, below Lake Sortedam, is the Blegdam area, where the Købke family moved in 1833.

it isn't that far from the city, whose spires are sometimes seen in the distance in the pictures of all four artists.

Købke's subject is what he, Christen Købke, sees as he wanders. His art is one of the products of the social and personal liberties of the era after Napoleon, but it should be said that Købke wasn't in revolt from another way of being an artist. His art is an informal record of his sensations because he was an heir to the new ideas and attitudes about nature and freedom and, also, because he simply made a lot of his most exciting work very much for himself. It was work done before his "career" started, when he was on the verge of being a "serious," professional artist.

Købke's sights were pretty much the same for the eight or so years when he was at his height. He painted the Citadel of Copenhagen (in Danish, Kastellet) and then the area around Lake Sortedam, at the time on the outskirts of Copenhagen. The Citadel was—and it remains today largely as it was then—a fortified bastion at the edge of the city, with the Øresund, the Sound, on one side of it. (Sweden is across the water.) While in no way prettified, the Citadel is a bit like a toy village in a children's story. It's surrounded by two levels of earth mounds, each in the shape of a star, with a moat in between. There are entryways on opposite ends, with stone gates, drawbridges, and woodwork painted the acidic rust red that one thinks of as "Købke red." Inside, along with the neatly arranged barracks and storehouses, there are a municipal building and a church. These face each other across a cobblestone street that goes the length of the bastion, from one entryway to the other.

Købke's paintings show the grass-covered mounds ringing the Citadel as a bright, friendly green; a cannon lies moldering in the grass, and there may be a ship on the Sound. Hans Edvard Norregård-Nielsen suggests that the Citadel, which included a few structures for conscripts and deserters, was something of a prison in Købke's time, and not a spanking clean one. We're told that Hans Christian Andersen, who set a story in the bastion, thought it a foul place. Købke, perhaps because he lived there from the age of seven through his early twenties and so couldn't be very objective about it, didn't touch on whatever grim aspects there might have been. In the few paintings set directly inside the Citadel, his subject was daily life. More often, he was looking beyond the place itself, out to the water or trees.

One of Købke's first paintings to have his particular razor-sharp,

Christen Købke, *View of the Square in the Citadel, Looking Toward the Embankment*, 1830. Oil on canvas, 11¾ × 9¼″ (30 × 23.5 cm). National Gallery of Scotland, Edinburgh.

light-filled realism—perhaps the first "Købke"—is also the only painting where he showed life within the bastion. In the gem-like *View of the Square in the Citadel, Looking Toward the Embankment* (pl. 4), we see three men who have come together, perhaps on a spring morning. The soft sunlight is so registered on the walls of the buildings that they look like a pound cake that's just been taken from the oven. The purest sunlight is seen in a thin, thin line of light touching the edge of a building. The scene feels as if it were being viewed from very far away, yet the three men are each firmly individualized, as is a man a little distance away who works at a well. Standing in profile, wearing a white shirt and tight leggings, he is poised in such a way that he might be transferred intact to a piece of Wedgwood pottery. Købke appears to have thought of him as a necessary element in a composition of considerable formal tension. It seems possible to estimate the number of feet separating him from the chatting threesome in overcoats.

The painter's father, Peter Berendt Købke, was the model for the man on the left. He's a formidable figure, and Peter Købke was formidable in life. He did well for himself as a baker in the early 1800s (his father and his grandfather had also been bakers). Then, after 1807, when Copenhagen was bombarded and set aflame by the British (the Danes were neutral at the time, and would later align themselves with Napoleon), he lost everything. After a number of years as a brewer, Peter returned to the bakery business, this time at the Citadel, where he and his wife and family moved in 1817. Peter and Cecilie Margrethe had eleven children, five girls and six boys, of whom Christen was the fifth. All lived to be adults.

Besides being industrious, Peter Købke was remembered as a good-natured employer (to a large staff) and an appreciator of his son and his son's many painter friends, a number of whom came to be family friends. The elder Købke also liked to pose, and besides the Citadel scene, Christen made quite a few drawings and oil portraits of him (pl. 46). Known as his father's companion on many walks, Christen actually was something of the nerve center or majordomo of the entire family. It was a large operation: in addition to the eleven children and, eventually, their spouses and their own children, various relatives were always drifting through. The painter seems to have been especially close to his sisters. He apparently had the same confiding relationship with some of them that he had with his fellow art students. He regularly used his sisters as models and made portraits of them—and of their husbands, who were often not so distantly related—and of his brothers. (The Købkes participated in a now unimaginable number of intermarriages.)

It has been noted that Købke had delicate health. He became interested in art when he needed something to do during a long illness when he was eleven, and he suffered a nervous stomach on and off for years. He apparently thought highly of cures for this or that; his favorite—he wanted everyone to do it—was a regime that included drinking glasses of cold water and taking daily cold baths. Købke was a small man even by the standards of his time. One of his nicknames was "the Little One." Another, probably based on his round cheeks, was "Bjørn" ("Bear"). An often reproduced oil portrait of him by his friend Wilhelm Marstrand, done in Italy, shows a somewhat phlegmatic, sweaty chap in a straw hat and scraggly full beard. The beard, though, was an experiment he made while away from home. In another Marstrand portrait, a drawing, and in one from his latter years by P. C. Skovgaard, as well as in Købke's powerful oil self-portrait done at the age of twenty-three (p. *viii*), we see an individual whose eyes and brain are fully alert—an image that tallies far more with the man we know from his own work.

Still, there is a good bit of Marstrand's Købke in Købke's letters. (They have survived, along with an almanac he kept for a short period, in copy form.) Year in and year out, we listen to an unfailingly earnest comrade. There isn't much temperament for a reader to grab hold of, except for one striking thing—an anxiousness about proving his worth. One of Købke's frequently quoted letters concerns his need to get a grip on himself, and elsewhere he presents his work as a sort of desperate endeavor, or writes about how he believes that God alone can help him. Our lasting impression may be of someone who hopes he can meet the challenge of his calling.

Christen Købke, *Self-Portrait*, 1829. Pencil, 5¾×4⅝" (14.6×11.6 cm). Kunstmuseum, Aarhus.

PORTRAITURE

Købke in his thoughts was often on an uphill climb, but Købke the painter was a natural. He was clearly a spectacular craftsman, and he matched the talents of his eyes and hand with something that isn't found in his letters—a psychological perceptiveness about people.

It's possible to believe that some ten to fifteen of Købke's portraits, done between 1831 and 1835, represent the pictures with which he takes a place alongside the cream of world painting. What makes them so distinctive? Corot made a number of portraits that are close to Købke's; they, too, are small, have a single-color background, and usually show the sitter from the chest up. (This description actually fits a host of portraits made at the time, from eastern Europe to the young United States.) Købke's portraits, though, are more than lovely. He looks at his sitters with a sympathy, a shrewdness, and a lucidity that can remind us of the way his near contemporary Keats, in his letters, talks about friends and acquaintances.

Købke presents some of the most memorable faces in European art of the period. His portrait of Johanne Pløyen (pl. 37) shows a bird-like old lady with a beamingly happy and alert face who clasps her eyeglasses. The fierce and brooding older man in *An Old Sailor* (pl. 10) seems to be surveying us with a look of reproachfulness. (Imagine a Dürer without the theatrically deranged quality.) His portrait of B. Høyen (pl. 24) presents a woman with dark hair, warm eyes, and an olive complexion who may be in her thirties. (She was the wife of the influential art historian and critic N. L. Høyen.) The touches of raspberry red and pink in her clothes enhance a note of sensual awareness and self-confidence in her eyes and lips. With the mirror-like perfection of the textures, and the seductiveness of the sitter, the portrait of Fru Høyen, small though it is, is as commanding as a contemporaneous portrait by Ingres.

Købke's portraits didn't come out of nowhere. A case might be

Christen Købke, *Christian Petersen*, 1833. Oil on canvas, 12⅜ × 10⅝″ (31.5 × 27 cm). Statens Museum for Kunst, Copenhagen.

made that portraiture was a strong suit of Danish art in the late eigh-
teenth and early nineteenth centuries. Jens Juel, one of the most
highly regarded Danish painters of the period before Eckersberg, is
the author of a slew of exquisite portraits, many in chalk, charcoal, and
pen and ink, and in the generation before Købke, C. A. Jensen estab-
lished himself as a master of the genre. Plain and simple in format, Jensen's portraits present actors, magistrates, matrons, young married
women—an entire society, it seems—all in what feel like ultimate
passport photos. Jensen has more than a passing resemblance to
Købke; in the 1830s, when Købke was at his height, some of his portraits are interchangeable with Jensen's.

In Købke's best portraits, however, the paint itself is felt, and there's
an overall tension, especially in the placement of the sitter within the
whole picture, that's way beyond Jensen. Christian Petersen (pl. 18), in
Købke's understatedly magnificent image of one of his brothers-in-
law (who was also a cousin), is a man who wears an onyx-like vest.
Købke includes just enough empty space on the sides of Petersen, and
the man's watery, somewhat sad gaze is so piercing, that his psyche
seems to vibrate in the narrow space surrounding him. Ida Thiele
(pl. 7), in Købke's close-up of a year-and-a-half-old child, has the
flattened-out and billowy appearance of an image caught with a tele-
photo lens or projected onto a background.

D. Christen Schifter Feilberg (pl. 40), another brother-in-law, is a
young man in a naval officer's uniform who turns to look at us in the
moment he's putting on a pale yellow glove. With its roomy and ex-
pansive air (it's basically a small picture), and its bright, clear colors,
and Feilberg's somewhat superior expression, this picture might be
seen alongside Degas. It sounds pejorative to say that it's also like a
fashion photograph a hundred years ahead of its time, but the portrait
happens to be that, too. Surely it's one of the more sensual images in
Danish painting.

Perhaps Købke's most emotional portrait is of the painter Lauritz

Christen Købke, *Ida Thiele*, 1832. Oil on
canvas, 8⅞ × 7⅞″ (22.5 × 20 cm). Statens
Museum for Kunst, Copenhagen.

Christen Købke, *Portrait of a Naval
Officer, D. Christen Schifter Feilberg*, 1834.
Oil on canvas, 20⅝ × 14¾″ (52.5 × 37.5
cm). Statens Museum for Kunst,
Copenhagen.

Lyngbye (pl. 29), an urgent young man with full lips and a little lump
on the side of his nose. The composition is unique in Købke's work and
in Danish art—perhaps in all European art. The sitter seems to be
coming out of the frame, up from the space behind it. The picture recalls those Early Renaissance portraits where the sitter looks out at the
viewer from behind a windowsill; but in the particular angles of Lyng-

bye's body and eyes there's a tension that isn't in earlier portraits and that hasn't dated one jot.

Lyngbye is the one Købke sitter who appears agitated. Købke the person, we feel, may have been a bit like his subject. Lyngbye embodies the controlled energy—the wrestled-over precision about light, color, and space—that underlies Købke's art.

ECKERSBERG

The portrait that probably brings viewers to Købke in the first place, however, is of another painter, Frederik Sødring (pl. 15). The art historian Vagn Poulsen called this portrait of a seated, friendly-looking, red-haired fellow the "most beautiful painting of Denmark's Golden Age." There is certainly a breathless perfection in the way every element in the picture—the presence and personality of the sitter; the classical proportions of the composition; the delectable painting of the background wall and the many different textures and materials we see; the cool grayish-green light pervading it all—comes together. The picture seems to show some quintessential Danish face. Sødring personifies what Danish writers of an earlier time, at least, listed as national characteristics: openness, conviviality, trustingness. Here is a portrait of a painter in his studio, which, by slightly enlarging the scope of the scene—by including a glimpse of his surrounding work area—leaves us with a sense of having entered and grasped the world he lived in.

There's nothing sugary, though, about the picture's image of ingenuousness and promise. Sødring at first appears to be a boy; on a second look he's clearly a young man, and he's as self-confident and humorous as he is sweet. His invitingly spread-legged, slouched position—it might have appealed to Caravaggio—holds our interest as much as his face does.

Christen Købke, *The Landscape Painter L. Lyngbye*, 1833. Oil on canvas, 10 ½ × 8 ½" (26.6 × 21.5 cm). Hirschsprungske Samling, Copenhagen.

Christen Købke, *The Landscape Painter F. Sødring*, 1832. Oil on canvas, 16 ⅝ × 14 ⅞" (42.2 × 37.9 cm). Hirschsprungske Samling, Copenhagen.

The painting's underlying subject, one can feel, is pride in being an artist. Sødring, whose specialty was landscape, is seen with palette and brush in hand; a painter's collapsible wood-and-leather sketching stool is off to the side. Prints are clipped to the wall behind him, and a bit of an easel can be seen in a mirror over his head. He sits surrounded by aspects of his trade as a young battlefront officer might be encircled by the fruits of victory.

The portrait might even be called a monument of sorts to the enterprise C. W. Eckersberg launched, the adventure of being a painting student in Copenhagen in the 1820s and 1830s. Sødring, unlike Købke, wasn't a student of Eckersberg's; yet both young men were clearly of the same world. (When the painting was made—it was a gift to Sødring on his twenty-third birthday—they shared a studio close to Charlottenborg and the Citadel.) And in many ways this world was Eckersberg's creation. Most of the best-known artists of the era were his students.

Eckersberg is sometimes referred to as the "father of Danish painting," and a certain sense of "fatherly" describes his work, which is intelligent and well intentioned, and not too arousing. There's an anonymous, inert quality to Eckersberg's art in general. Yet he isn't negligible. A number of his pictures have a beckoning pale, frosty light. Open to every new idea of his day, he can engage us—often by his sheer choice of subject—even when his individual picture overall is far from momentous. And it's hard not to be drawn to Eckersberg when the subject is Købke, because the very elements that molded Købke's work come from Eckersberg (and come fairly intact).

A short, compact man, Eckersberg appears in portraits by Jensen and others as kindly, brisk, and self-contained. A key moment in his early life came when, after his academic study was over in Copenhagen, he didn't take the usual route to Rome but went instead to Paris. There, for part of his stay, which lasted from 1810 through 1813, he was a student of Jacques-Louis David, premier painter to the emperor and perhaps the most illustrious art teacher of the day. Eckersberg eventually spent three years in Rome, and by 1818 he was a professor at Charlottenborg, where he would remain (he and his family lived in the building, too) until his death, in 1853. He kept a detailed diary for most of his years, so we know the very day when this student appeared, that one left. He loved music, and he outlived his two wives—both daughters of Jens Juel.

Eckersberg's work is unusually various (this fact may be connected with his being a gifted teacher). He brought back views of sites from Rome, and he added to them landscapes, family scenes, portraits, and religious, historical, and mythological costume dramas. There are informal scenes of city folk running along a bridge at night, laborers hanging around a shipyard, gentry out for a stroll on a summer evening. Finally, there are marines. Danish writers point with pleasure at Eckersberg's ship scenes, believing that in them he painted what was closest to his affections.

Eckersberg was an artist at a crossroad. In his work the formulas and grand designs of eighteenth-century art, with its tinkling, cool, and mandarinish conceptions, and its porcelain coating, give way. The possibilities of a realism of his own time are opened up—and Eckersberg steps cautiously into that new realism. We're not sure whether it is more striking that he wanted to make an art about the people and places of his own time or that he was so stiff and cautious about it.

Maybe Eckersberg's woodenness can be explained by his having two passions—which he couldn't quite bring together. He was devoted to perspective, a subject he wrote two books about and strongly encouraged his students to learn and use. At the same time, he urged his students to draw from nature; being true to nature, he said, meant being faithful to observable reality, to what is really before our eyes. Eckersberg seems almost to have advocated that randomness play a

C. W. Eckersberg, *Ideal View of Charlottenborg and the Residence of the Gardener of the Botanical Gardens, Seen from Nyhavn's North Side*, c. 1845. Black ink, and gray wash over pencil, 11 ⅜ × 9 ¾" (28.8 × 24.9 cm). Kongelige Kobberstiksamling, Statens Museum for Kunst, Copenhagen.

part in the process of making a picture, so that paintings would more closely resemble the way we actually see things. These precepts resulted (in his own work) in paintings that resemble all too lucidly laid-out stage sets on which various figures, each as natural as, say, a statuette on a trophy, and with facial expressions that seem carved, and that range from the alarmed to the glum, are placed. Eckersberg's pictures without people—a deserted waterfront; a cloister in Rome—can be fairly impressive. He liked finding serene formal balances in the world at large (he would have made a good de Stijl artist). But even in his finest paintings some sense of real light, some crispness, is missed.

In many of his drawings, however, Eckersberg's ideas flowed together. A quiet shipyard; citizens walking along a street; a lamplighter at work; girls at a window; sunny public squares—these are some of his images. Nothing is especially personal, private, or urgent (and the figures aren't much better than they are in his paintings), but we're pleased by Eckersberg's range of soft shadings, his feeling for shadows, and especially, his sense of how much white, untouched paper he can use (for, say, water). He makes Copenhagen an elegant and spooky place. We're left thinking about the surprising correspondences between these drawings and Renaissance ideal cityscapes, or de Chirico, or Minimal art.

Købke's achievement was that, in the early 1830s, when he was first becoming a mature artist, he made a natural, breathing connection between the poles of Eckersberg's teaching—between rules and everyday subject matter. In his best portraits, with their sense of being about the painter's particular distance from the sitter at a precise moment, and in his small views of the area around the Citadel—pictures of clouds, sky, distant sea, ramparts, faraway ship masts, and the odd wandering, yet wonderfully placed, person—Købke took Eckersberg's ideas into real-life air and light.

In his other pictures of the time, of individuals in a setting (such as *View of the Square in the Citadel, Looking Toward the Embankment* [pl. 4]), Købke seems more purely experimental than in his portraits or views. Most of these paintings are of a single figure in a specific place. In *Portion of the Plaster Cast Collection at Charlottenborg* (p. *ii*), a man, a piece of cloth in his hand, bends over to look closely at a cast. *A View from a Storehouse in the Citadel* (pl. 6) shows a girl in a bonnet walking up a ramp, toward the viewer. In *The Cigar Seller by the Northern Gate of the Citadel* (pl. 5), an ominous older man sits by a table on a path leading out to water. In other pictures we see a woman in a living room or a nude male model posing in an art class (pl. 22). Købke's subject, it

Christen Købke, *A View from a Storehouse in the Citadel*, 1831. Oil on canvas, 15 3/8 × 12" (39 × 30.5 cm). Statens Museum for Kunst, Copenhagen.

seems, is the construction of a measured indoor or outdoor space, where the figure is used a bit impersonally, although not inertly, as was often the case with Eckersberg. Købke's vacant-yet-tense scenes recall Piero della Francesca—his *Flagellation*, for instance—in that we feel we're looking at flesh-and-blood people who have been commanded by the painter, at this moment, "Freeze!"

In *A View from a Storehouse*, the girl walking up the ramp, her eyes downcast, is clearly thinking about something other than what she's looking at. (The model was one of Købke's sisters.) What's also immediately felt is that the little boys at the bottom of the ramp are entranced by her. She, of course, doesn't know this. And neither the girl nor the boys know that they're being watched by the artist, or by us—by whoever is looking out of the storehouse. Some Danes think *A View* is among Købke's very best pictures. However high one ranks it, it's certainly a tour de force on his abiding theme—looking.

Is there a connection between Købke's "scene" pictures, which might be illustrations for a wide range of children's books, and the fact that Købke was a contemporary of his countryman Andersen and of his near-neighbors, the north German Brothers Grimm? Are we looking at, in effect, the first children's book illustrations? The questions only add to the mysteriousness and charm of the pictures.

DANISH PAINTERS

Danish painting from the 1820s to the 1840s came to be recognized and admired in the late nineteenth century in the excitement surrounding the new French Impressionist and Post-Impressionist art. Danish writers of the time (and up to the period after the First World War) believed that the earlier Danish painters and modern painters shared a similar intimate, spontaneous response to nature and a similar lack of rhetoric, "literature," grand designs. People today, I think, enjoy most of these painters—among the better known of whom are Martinus Rørbye, P. C. Skovgaard, Constantin Hansen, Jørgen Roed, Dankvart Dreyer, and Wilhelm Marstrand—in the same way. It's in their sketch-like, of-the-moment landscapes, or their studies of an odd building by a road, or an old church, that Købke's contemporaries are most alive.

There are lovely nature studies in particular by Skovgaard and Dreyer, who were primarily landscapists. And much pleasure can be had in looking at drawings by many of these artists. Marstrand, whose sketches (from memory) of Kierkegaard as he walked through the streets of Copenhagen are considered the truest likenesses of the man, made numerous scratchy, satiric drawings of the Danish middle class making itself look foolish that can be put beside images by Hogarth and Daumier.

When the painters became more ambitious, though, when they tried to paint significant scenes of their own time, or historical dramas, they fell flat. Many of the characteristic and ambitious pictures of Rørbye, Roed, and Hansen are nebulous. Even the paintings of Marstrand, who was long considered the preeminent nineteenth-century Danish painter, chiefly because of his flickering, open brushwork, are more artifacts of the time.

Yet there was a theme that clearly excited many of the Golden Age painters. It was their experience as students, or student life itself. There was an extreme sense of community among these young artists, and they inched into the terrain of making art about it. One of Marstrand's more engaging pictures is of a group of young men assembled at night, around candles, and Købke, besides his portrait of Sødring with his painter's equipment, and another of Marstrand at his easel (pl. 1), made an especially fine drawing of Eckersberg and Marstrand on a painting expedition (pl. 14).

One of the most absorbing pictures of the era is Constantin Hansen's *A Group of Danish Artists in Rome*. Informal but tense, it's a quietly dramatic scene of seven men seated or standing in a room, with large open French windows, and a placid spaniel plopped in a chair, regarding the men. It is less a wonderful painting—it's conventionally conceived—than a wonderful document. Hansen shows what probably was a part of the experience for many Scandinavians in Rome: their isolation within the Mediterranean community. Here are our northern bachelors, listening to a heavyset man—the architect Gottlieb

Constantin Hansen, *A Group of Danish Artists in Rome*, 1837. Oil on canvas, 24½ × 29⅛″ (62.3 × 74 cm). Statens Museum for Kunst, Copenhagen.

Bindesbøll, who's talking about his recent travels to Greece—but really, it seems, they are lost in their own thoughts.

Some of the men smoke the enormously long pipes of the time; one man, Hansen himself, looks carefully at another. Rørbye, who possesses an oddly elongated face, is absorbed with a cup and saucer, twisting his fingers around them. He seems to be at the center of the picture's many little stories. Art circles in Copenhagen at the time suspected that Hansen was showing a Rørbye who was plainly bored with having to hear Bindesbøll's stories again. But to a general viewer, Rørbye is doing more intensely what nearly everyone else in the picture is doing, that is, listening somewhat, but mostly thinking—What will it be like when I go home? Will anyone there appreciate the changes Italy has made in me? Have there been any changes?

The image, or theme, of young men coming together was really seized by Wilhelm Bendz, perhaps the most engaging Danish painter of the time besides Købke. Bendz isn't an easy artist to get a sense of. When he died—at twenty-eight—he was still experimenting with widely different approaches (he was something of an experimenter all along). He began studying with Eckersberg before the teacher's other well-known pupils, and one has a feeling that Bendz was never as much a pure student of Eckersberg as the others. Bendz did so many different kinds of paintings in his short lifetime there's no way to categorize him. But he had a special feeling for nighttime scenes of groups of young men in artificially lit rooms, with shadows playing wild games on the walls. There's a major painting of students zooming about in a candelit life class at an art school, and another of bohemian artists and students carrying on in a Munich beer hall. In a third painting, young gents have gathered one night in a Copenhagen apartment to smoke, play musical instruments, and sing.

If you enjoy putting your hands together and creating silhouettes on the wall, you'll probably want to study these pictures. Most viewers will simply need an extra amount of time to figure out what they're looking at. Where is that preposterous shadow coming from? How much is the artist exaggerating in order to achieve it? How did Bendz actually paint these scenes? These dark-yet-streaky pictures seem far afield from the staid Eckersberg and his precepts about nature and the

Wilhelm Bendz, *A Smoking Party*, 1828.
Oil on canvas, 38¾ × 33½" (98.5 × 85 cm).
Ny Carlsberg Glyptotek, Copenhagen.

natural. Yet Bendz's partying young men surely derive from the enterprise Eckersberg set in motion. Centering on the idea of fantastic shadows, Bendz found a metaphor—a purely visual metaphor, one that couldn't work in the form of writing or music—for the theme of young artists coming together, enlarging and transforming themselves.

Bendz also made a number of good portraits. Some are charmingly stiff works on the order of American folk art of the 1830s, while others—a self-portrait with a guitar, for example—convey a sense of a mystery to be solved by the viewer. In Garmisch-Partenkirchen, on his way to Italy (where he died), he painted a small picture of a man seen from the rear in a coach house, possibly at night. The way the overlapping arches, in subtly related shades of gray, envelop the slim, distant, leaning figure, has an elegance and a complexity that recall the Dutch architectural painter Pieter Saenredam, and may be unmatched in Danish painting.

There remains one final contribution by Bendz, a little piece of magic that effortlessly takes us back to the Copenhagen of those days.

Wilhelm Bendz, *Interior from Amaliegade, with the Artist's Brothers*, c. 1830. Oil on canvas, 12¾ × 19¼″ (32.3 × 49 cm). Hirschsprungske Samling, Copenhagen.

It is an interior, showing two young men (his brothers) in an apartment in the Amaliegade, a street near Amalienborg, the royal palace. One fellow is at a stand-up desk at the side of the room, lost in thought. Across from him, seated on a sofa, engaged in his studies, is another, rather chunky man. We might be looking at the first moment of a theater piece, or a ballet. The curtain has gone up and in an instant something will happen. What makes the picture a particularly Biedermeier classic is that the hero of the piece, so to speak, is the room itself. The walls are a distinct shade of blue-green, with a good bit of white separating them, and this wonderfully pleasing color duet makes the painting sing out from a distance. Bendz's Amaliegade picture has probably delighted more viewers than any of the Danish Golden Age except Købke's portrait of Sødring. (They're both in the Hirschsprung Collection in Copenhagen, where they hang facing each other.)

The other arresting figure of the period is Johan Thomas Lundbye. He didn't study with Eckersberg, and he pointedly did not share the professor's interests. Eight years Købke's junior, he represents the wave of new attitudes that came in after Købke. Lundbye stares out with the look of an angry and wounded young man in his self-portrait; and his small portraits of his parents are very different from Købke's portraits of his, which are as full of sympathy and respect as an eye for character. Unusual in Danish pictures of the time, Lundbye's parents have not altogether pleasant faces. They're like the glum and sourish combatants in a Strindberg play.

Lundbye, who also grew up in the Citadel, studied informally with Købke for a period, and passages in various diaries and letters show that the two liked and admired one another. But a diary entry from the time of Købke's death implies another story. "Let me be honest," Lundbye writes, "in dealing with the noblest of feelings. There are only a few—none but my mother in my family, and outside it not many—whose death would be a painful loss to me. Købke could not be counted among them." Lundbye's pictures resemble this sharp-tongued remark. They are tantalizing; they have a presence—but not enough is delivered.

Lundbye's landscapes, his predominant work, are painted with bright, pleasingly acidic colors. The local boys and girls who populate some of these scenes can have engagingly stiff, weird bodies and faces. Lundbye is conspicuous among Danish painters of the time for brushing on oil paint in fluid, sensuous ways; he had the touch, in miniature, of one of the bravura painterly painters of the late nineteenth century. His finest pictures are like diminutive Oriental screens. A very small painting in the Hirschsprung of a pond, with two wood planks, each a different bright color, sticking into the water, is one of the loveliest of all Danish paintings.

But Lundbye never developed his sense of touch and his feeling for

Johan Thomas Lundbye, *View of a Pond.* Oil on paper, mounted on canvas, 6 × 8⅞" (15.4 × 22.4 cm). Hirschsprungske Samling, Copenhagen.

color into a larger style. He seems to have been as engaged by politics as by art. A voluminous manifesto-writer and diary-keeper (he noted Kierkegaard's developing thought), he had a program behind his choice of subjects. When he painted scenes of what the art historian Henrik Bramsen calls the "then deserted, wild, and unknown northern Zealand"—the island on which Copenhagen is situated—he expected his fellow Danes to be stirred. (Jutland, the part of the nation connected with mainland Europe, was at the time a far less familiar part of Denmark to the people of Copenhagen.) But when Lundbye made good-sized, even enormous, pictures of a grand and idyllic homeland, he lost his sketch-artist's flair, and he didn't replace it with anything. A viewer quits Lundbye's company with the thought that this man was too talented and too smart to have made his protagonist a distant cow.

FREDERIKSBORG

Describing the era after Napoleon's rise to dominance, an era that continued for some time after Waterloo, in 1815, art historians speak about a Romantic Nationalism in art. It was a belief in the physical beauty and distinctiveness of one's fatherland and a conviction that this was a fitting subject for art.

Lundbye was a prime mover in the Danish branch of this movement. Købke, whose aims were set some years before the idea took hold and whose pictures were done in a more analytical spirit, isn't strictly considered a Romantic Nationalist. But for a non-Danish viewer of his work now, Købke is the definition of a Danish painter. In the unusual small sizes of his pictures and the modesty and undramatic nature of his subjects, his art epitomizes the more outward, apparent sense Danes have of themselves. And in his images of Frederiksborg Castle—there are roughly nine paintings (in a wide range of sizes) and many drawings— Købke touches another side of the Danish character: the pride of a small country in having maintained a distinct identity for so long.

The idea of painting a national treasure (such as the early-seventeenth-century Frederiksborg) certainly wasn't Købke's. It was N. L. Høyen, with his battle plan for all Danish painters, who proclaimed historic buildings urgent subjects. And some of the best paintings of the era, including works by Hansen and Lundbye, are of various churches and castles. It was Høyen himself who drew Købke's attention to Frederiksborg.

In its size and breadth, Frederiksborg, which is in Hillerød, less than half an hour by car from Copenhagen, is one of the major castles of Scandinavia. This is somehow an un-Danish thing to be (the scale of buildings is generally small in Denmark), yet the castle, comprising three island-like units and set entirely in a man-made body of water, presents itself with a very Danish understated gracefulness. Hillerød today is a somewhat modernized large town, and its buildings sit in relation to the castle in the same retiring way they do in Købke's pictures. In his time Hillerød was about a half-day's carriage ride from Copenhagen. Did the unadventurous Købke miss a home-cooked meal when he painted Frederiksborg? No. His sister Conradine and her husband, Nikolai Feilberg, a pastor, lived there. Købke stayed with them during parts of the summers of 1834 and 1835, when he tackled the subject. It might be noted that he worked on other pictures at the time, too, and the castle appears in his work, usually as a backdrop, on and off throughout the thirties.

Købke's first Frederiksborg images are two views from the castle's roof. He made each in his characteristically small sizes, and then again in versions that, at about five feet square, are among his largest works. The various drawings for these views are remarkable. If part of Købke's contribution to world painting is his ability to catch that particular moment when light creeps into the atmosphere and starts dissolving the edges of forms, then these drawings might be considered the essence of his contribution.

In one of the views we look at a turret, beyond which are fields and woods and then sky (pl. 43). A stork stands on a nearby chimney, and another one, wings outstretched—it isn't immediately visible—flies off into the distance. Very, very far away, people are strolling. The other image, in the large version, is strangely devoid of faraway bits (pl. 44). We look at a lone brick chimney and the ridge of a roof, with a view off into the distance. It's like a detail from a larger picture, chosen perversely for its unusual lack of interest.

Then, in the summer of 1835, Købke tried a panoramic view of the castle, this time at sunset, and he wasn't as successful. He made a lovely small oil study for this postcard-like image (pl. 45), and there exist a number of spruce preparatory drawings. But the large version shows the artist running along, panting, behind an overblown and impersonal conception. This dryly painted work makes us think primarily of the tediousness for a painter of having to account for the castle's innumerable windows. If Købke had been less a poet he would have had less of a problem with the job.

He wasn't tired of Frederiksborg, though. On his third try, this time painting the building from the northwest, he was back in form. Like the rooftop views, this image, which exists as a very full oil sketch (pl. 49) and a silkily smooth larger, finished work (pl. 53), has a pleasing casualness. The castle, set on the right side of the picture, is something of a backdrop to a scene that includes a tree bending in the wind and rushes bending in the water, and some tourists making their way into the castle. Købke's craftsmanship is on parade in these pictures; each detail is felt for itself and as paint.

In the end, we come back to the rooftop scenes. They may not have

Christen Købke, *One of the Turrets at Frederiksborg Castle*, 1834–35. Oil on canvas, 69⅝ × 63¾″ (177 × 162 cm). Danske Kunstindustrimuseum, Copenhagen.

the fullness or intensity of the best Købkes, but in their large versions they're his most audacious pictures. In his view of the lone and ordinary chimney, set against a vast, empty, strikingly bland sky, Købke took Eckersberg's ideas about a new everyday realism to the breaking point; he was a step away from making a picture of atmosphere itself. And in his view of the tower with its spire, Købke sneaked up on the Romantic Nationalists and beat them at their own game. His wit lies in focusing on an aspect of Frederiksborg that uniquely suggests national pride. There probably isn't another Danish painting that conveys so deftly the sense of a presiding place, a structure that holds do-

Christen Købke, *The Roof of Frederiksborg Castle, with a View Toward Lake, Town, and Woods*, 1834–35. Oil on canvas, 69⅝ × 67⅜″ (177 × 171 cm). Danske Kunstindustrimuseum, Copenhagen.

minion over the land. (Danes seem particularly fond of spires. To this day the many spires of Copenhagen, each with its own character, together form one of the city's most distinctive features.)

The Frederiksborg rooftop paintings in their large, squarish versions recall a few other similarly sized pictures that present a wide-open view of the world. These include a number of paintings that Canaletto made during his stay in England, particularly two views of the Thames from Richmond House, and Pieter Saenredam's largest and most extraordinary painting—a view, looking toward the ceiling, of the interior of St. Bavo Church in Haarlem. Here are disparate works—an Italian painter's images of England of the 1740s; a Dutch painting of the 1640s; and Danish paintings of the 1830s—that somehow form a category of their own within the history of art. Presenting aspects of buildings and vast open space, they're about the experience of looking. Each is by a painter who worked in an unspontaneous, carefully planned manner, in generally small sizes, and with images that demand an intense peering. Here that painter is stepping back, picking up his head from his close-up work; yet he has geared every element to the smallest detail, so the pictures, when they're felt, are engulfing.

THE DINING ROOM

There remains one more strand to the story of Købke at Frederiksborg. When he started to paint the castle seriously, in the latter months of 1833, he had recently moved with his family from the Citadel to an area a little farther beyond the city. This was the Blegdam (or "bleaching grounds"), situated on the distant side of one of the city's outlying lakes. These man-made lakes had supplied drinking water for Copenhagen for centuries. Nowadays their shorelines are fairly straight and they're bordered by offices and apartment buildings. Set within metropolitan Copenhagen, they look quite like reservoirs. In Købke's time, though, their shores were irregular; the lakes were the beginning of the rural or suburban outskirts of the city. Along the water were good-sized homes and gentlemen's farms, and gardens and trees, often with little piers and boats. Looking back toward Copenhagen from the far side of the lakes, one saw the city's windmills, ships' masts, and spires in the distance.

The painter was twenty-three when his family, including his unmarried sisters and some of his brothers, along with a number of servants, moved to a large new house by Lake Sortedam. Peter Købke, writes Kasper Monrad, had just retired from his bakery concession a wealthy man. Within a year of moving, his son was at work on a suite

Christen Købke, *Night (after Thorvaldsen's relief)*, 1834–35. Oil on canvas, 29⅞ × 29⅞″ (76 × 76 cm). Davids Samling, Copenhagen.

Christen Købke, *Day (after Thorvaldsen's relief)*, 1834–35. Oil on canvas, 29⅞ × 29⅞″ (76 × 76 cm). Davids Samling, Copenhagen.

of four decorative pictures for a large formal dining room in the house. Two of them were his large rooftop paintings of Frederiksborg (pls. 43, 44).

Was it Købke himself who initiated the idea of making decorations for the dining room? Did the very nature of dining room decorations predict the uneventful, screen-like quality of these pictures? Perhaps Købke believed that if he filled canvases this size with his usual mass of fine details, the images would be overwhelmingly full of things to look at. Whatever the answers, the Frederiksborg rooftop pictures are best seen—and they have a different meaning when they're seen—along with the two other pictures Købke painted for the room. Viewed together, as a decorative ensemble, the four works form a sort of headquarters of his art, though one where he put his thoughts in an indirect way.

The other paintings in the scheme were *Day* and *Night* (pls. 41, 42), copies of circular marble low-relief carvings by Bertel Thorvaldsen. Each emblematic image—they were among Thorvaldsen's best-known re-creations of classical art—is of a goddess in flight. The goddess of the Day, scattering flowers before her, effortlessly sails along, a child—the spirit of Light—on her shoulders. The goddess of the Night, accompanied by an owl, carries her children—Sleep and Death—in her arms. Købke's circular pictures are in grisaille (in shades of gray), and they're surprises. In few other paintings do we see his hand, his brushwork, so clearly. And *Night*, where the goddess' head is bowed, is unexpectedly affecting. These are among the rare works where the art of the classical world has been made over into something fresh—maybe because Købke wasn't working directly from classical art but from Thorvaldsen's pastiches.

A drawing by Købke gives an idea of how the room probably looked. *Day* and *Night* were each to be hung in the center of a wall, and each was to flank a double door. Each tondo was placed on a painted squarish background. The backgrounds corresponded roughly with the rooftop pictures in size, suggesting that these views were hung, in a formally balanced way, opposite *Day* and *Night*. What else was in the room isn't known; some scholars believe that the four pictures might have been arranged somewhat differently.

The dining room pictures, taken individually or as a group, aren't very highly regarded by Danes. Emil Hannover set the prevailing note when he commented that there was nothing to discuss about them as works of art. And as each pair is owned by a different Copenhagen museum, and *Day* and *Night* weren't reproduced in the standard catalogue of Købke's work, of 1915—and as the paintings have rarely been reproduced since—a viewer has to do some mental appreciation on his own to reunite the four pictures. Yet with Købke's sketch of the one wall before us, we can imagine them together. The rooftop pictures suddenly become, like the tondos, inseparable mates; and the two sets of pale, hyper-controlled colors—the silver-grays of the tondos; the olive-tans, reds, and blacks of the views—are a surprising and suave combination.

It's not known how, or whether, the four pictures dominated the room. But surely they had more weight than four grace notes. Købke might very well have planned the entire room, especially the relation of the background wall colors to his paintings. He was very conscious in all his art at the time about placing, as it were, certain colors in unexpected relationship to others. The walls in his studio and his own room in the new house were arranged in particular colors by his friend Georg Hilker, a decorative painter. (The walls were dark red in the studio, gray in his room.) Picturing the dining room, we see an unusual

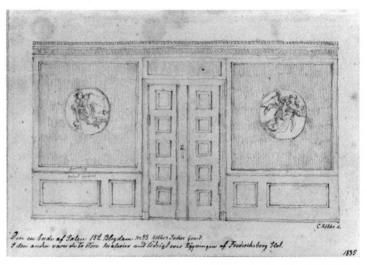

Christen Købke, *End-wall in the Dining Room of Købke's Parents' House*, 1835. Pencil, 5½ × 8⅛" (14 × 20.6 cm). Danske Kunstindustrimuseum, Copenhagen. The drawing shows how Købke thought of placing his *Night* and *Day* tondos on the dining room wall in the family's new house at Blegdamsvej 15. It's worth noting that the rectangles on which the circular paintings are placed aren't the same size (the right is slightly wider). This subtle difference enhances the connection between these Neoclassical pictures and the two other pictures in the room, the Frederiksborg Castle views—because one of these views is slightly wider than the other.

array of muted and glistening tones. Købke becomes purely and simply the expert designer. It's oddly bracing to think of him being only partially concerned with the Romantic Nationalism bound up with Frederiksborg, or with the Neoclassicism of Thorvaldsen's pastiches.

The artist doesn't talk about the project in his surviving letters, and it isn't likely that he was telling a story with the pictures. But looking at the two pairs as arbitrarily or casually chosen, as space-fillers, makes no sense. How could Købke have wanted his family and friends and colleagues not to intuit connections? He certainly seems to be showing movement and time in both pairs. The titles *Day* and *Night* spell out opposites, or change, and the images themselves show gentle and steady lifting movements in different directions. The rooftop pictures represent movement, too; they show shifting viewpoints of someone standing on the castle's roof.

Perhaps because we connect the goddesses carrying babies with the storks, the pictures together suggest the subject of parenthood, and of the movement, the very process, of life. The storks are goddess-like themselves. Viscerally, at least, the four pictures together become a sort of meditation on the passage of time, on being brought into the world and being taken out of it. If we're led to think that this was Købke's underlying theme, it's because we know the pictures were done for a family room by a son, and because an underlying story of this son's life was his closeness to his family.

Christen Købke, *Storks*. Pencil, 5 3/8 × 4″ (13.8 × 10.3 cm). Kongelige Kobberstiksamling, Statens Museum for Kunst, Copenhagen.

TROUBLES

The year after he moved with his family to their new house, Købke began to face real challenges, and real difficulties, in being an artist. He continued for a while to make highly finished portrait drawings and small oil portraits of family and friends, and he had no problem with them. But many writers, including Henrik Bramsen and Hans Edvard

Norregård-Nielsen, note the experimental nature, the ambitiousness, and the frustration of these years, particularly the period from late 1835 to sometime in 1837. We hear about a painter who increasingly wanted to go deeper in his work and to apologize for his earlier art, which was seen as "materialistic," as lacking in "idealism"—in a large, propelling idea. Part of Købke's desire to be clearer about his convictions surely also came from the fact that he was going to be a husband. (Perhaps part of what made the period one of genuine development came from this fact, too.) In the spring of 1836 he became engaged to Susanne Cecilie Købke (pl. 62), a cousin who was his age, twenty-six, and in November 1837, he and Sanne, as she was called, were married.

The effort to go beyond the private, "little" life he had been leading in his work was considerable, and commentators have long been divided about the results of that effort. *View Outside the North Gate of the Citadel* (pl. 36), for example, his first really public work, a commission from the Kunstforening (Art Association), has continually drawn an ambivalent response. This 1834 view from one of the Citadel's entryways at a sunny and uncrowded moment, with a few people here and there on a bridge, teeters between greatness and emptiness. An inseparable blend of *La Grande Jatte* and Currier and Ives, it's a picture that, whether the artist quite intended it or not, sums up a place and a time in its Sunday best. It is also a generic nineteenth-century image, a work by no artist in particular that you walk right by in a museum.

The painting becomes engrossing when we look closely at the scene and discover a man in a top hat and a woman in a blue dress, walking at the far end of the bridge. Half of the woman is missing because, from our point of view, part of the bridge is in front of her. Realizing that Købke is being playfully precise about where he's standing in order to see this particular scene, we find ourselves viewing the whole picture more attentively. The two massive brick gates that frame the scene,

Wilhelm Marstrand, *Portrait of Christen Købke*, 1836. Pencil, 5 ⅜ × 4 ⅞″ (13.5 × 12.3 cm). Kongelige Kobberstiksamling, Statens Museum for Kunst, Copenhagen.

Christen Købke, *View Outside the North Gate of the Citadel*, 1834. Oil on canvas, 31⅛ × 36⅝″ (79 × 93 cm). Ny Carlsberg Glyptotek, Copenhagen.

and the very particular shadows everywhere, give the picture an attractive Poussin-like air of immobility. Some oars, beautifully colored in themselves, are stacked in a lovely shadowy area near one wall—they only gradually reveal themselves. And the boys on the bridge, precursors of the lounging locals that Winslow Homer would put in his pictures forty years later, might have been positioned by a choreographer. (A superb pencil study of the boys exists [pl. 35].) Yet we hear ourselves admiring the picture. The half-seen woman, the bit of life that sparks our interest, is like a heart that is too small for the body it's placed in.

Købke's large *Østerbro in Morning Light* (pl. 52), a work completed two years later, is similar to *North Gate* in that we have to peer into it before it becomes alive. And like *North Gate* it was a major undertaking. Not that Købke knew of Vermeer, but this was to be his *View of Delft*. Here is a panoramic view of a street with many windswept poplars—the site was not many feet from the Købke family house on Blegdamsvej—that presents a highly specific light and a carefully worked-out perspective, for which he made numerous preparatory drawings (pl. 50). There are also many rather individualized people going about their business, and there are cows, too. Købke hadn't painted cows before, and he warmed up with some charming pencil sketches of them (pl. 51).

Østerbro in Morning Light is certainly esteemed in Denmark. But few writers over the years have really embraced it. Up close, when we look in, especially at the street level, the picture is alive. We're pleased when we discover people walking along in the shade on the right (Kierkegaard lived on this street for a while in his last years); we wish that Købke had made a vast painting only of street life. Moving back from the picture, though, we lose sight of the people and are left with mostly trees and sky. The work seems undernourished. It has more sweat and preparation than innards.

Emil Hannover thought that when Købke turned to God in his letters, the emotion came from being too much in his head, too introspective or melancholic. Hannover didn't quite believe in Købke's own religious belief. He was probably on the mark in questioning it. Købke's expressions of piety generally coincided with periods when he was having difficulties with work. But a reader of his letters might also feel that Købke had a fairly religious apprehension of things—that by nature he was given to thinking that God, or someone, or something, was over his shoulders, judging him. And periodically throughout his life—the note is heard from his earliest letters through the very last ones—he expressed a longing to divest himself of things, to be recharged spiritually, to operate with the chastened strength of one of Christ's disciples.

Whether out of fearfulness or because he was going deeper into himself, Købke, especially in the time after his engagement, turned to evangelical sermons and poetry with pious overtones. In the writing about him, we also encounter a Købke who may have been searching for a mentor at this point. He had put himself under the tutelage of Eckersberg and then Høyen, at earlier moments. Did Købke, in 1836, become a protégé of H. E. Freund because it was time to move on to a new mentor, or because he had to get Eckersberg (and Høyen) out of his system? The answer is probably a bit of both.

Hermann Ernst Freund is a slippery figure in Købke's story and in the story of Danish art of the time. He was a sculptor, a man of apparently some ambition when he studied under Thorvaldsen in Rome in the early 1820s. He had hoped at one point to carry the mantle of a new spirit in art; he had aspirations to present sculpture about Nordic gods, not the classical past (Thorvaldsen's terrain). But Freund appears to have embraced his own Nordic heritage more because it was not what Thorvaldsen was doing than because he was attracted to it for itself. He was actually quite content to make and to advocate art about the classical world; but where Thorvaldsen specialized in big, flawlessly carved marble showstoppers, Freund was more involved with Hellenistic decoration.

Freund won a Copenhagen prize for a commission while in Rome, but the work couldn't be finished as he intended, and on his return to

C. A. Jensen, *H. E. Freund*, 1835. Oil on canvas, 11⅜ × 8⅝" (29 × 22 cm). Ny Carlsberg Glyptotek, Copenhagen.

Denmark in the late 1820s (Thorvaldsen still holding forth in Rome), he had problems with other projects, too. In the next decade, now a professor at the Academy, Freund became a presence in the Danish art scene. While in public he was retiring, he presided easily enough at his home and workplace, the Materialgården, which, decorated in the Pompeiian manner, was an open house.

What thoughts passed between Freund and Købke can't be pinned down precisely, but Købke mentions Freund in letters beginning in the summer of 1835, and a year later he talks about the man in a way that suggests a real closeness. Hannover thought that Freund had a severely damaging influence on Købke, that he encouraged the painter to abandon the instinctive spirit of his early art. Not everyone has agreed. And it's worth noting, if only to give a sense of the art scene at the moment, that Købke wasn't the only artist his age or younger who spent time with the barely active sculptor, and that Høyen was very much a part of the discussion at Freund's gatherings. But it makes sense that Købke, who had probably used up Eckersberg and who had a propensity to worry, would be drawn into the orbit of a man who both promised a new vision of art and seemed to pass his days in a state of melancholic semi-retirement.

What Købke's portraits of Freund (pls. 63–65) suggest is that the sculptor was an important and stimulating figure to him. Arne Brenna, the authority on the subject, has pointed out that Købke didn't make portraits of Eckersberg or Høyen. Freund actually may have been something of a charmer, or a gadfly, in his person. He appears somewhat like this in two appealing portraits by C. A. Jensen. In one, made when he was a young student in Rome, he has a delicate and bony face and wears a large floppy beret; in the other, done in Copenhagen when he was in his forties, he seems a sincere and debonair fellow. And in sketches of him sitting and listening, or at work, by various artists including Eckersberg and Købke, he looks like an impatient ad-

Christen Købke, *H. E. Freund Sitting on a Sofa*. Pencil, 5 ½ × 4″ (13.9 × 10.2 cm). Kongelige Kobberstiksamling, Statens Museum for Kunst, Copenhagen.

olescent. But in two magnificent drawings—a worked-out study for a large, full-figure oil, and a study of Freund's head alone—Købke saw a rugged, sensuous, and crestfallen individual. These drawings, among the most powerful Købke did, attest to how much he saw in the older man.

There's a lot to admire in Købke's large oil painting, too. Freund is shown in the Hellenistic smock and slippers he generally wore, sitting before a wall that is a stern brick-red, with odd and mysterious Pompeiian details here and there on the wall and floor. It's generally thought that his pose, his body and head subtly downcast, conveys self-centeredness and an inability to act. And yes, the general note is of someone who waits, listens, thinks. But Købke also conveys (especially to a viewer who hasn't heard of Freund) a sense of a prepossessing figure—a deity, almost—in repose.

If the portrait isn't one of Købke's best pictures, if it fails to stay in the mind, it may be because Freund's face is undeveloped emotionally and overcooked technically, as painting. There's a discrepancy between the sheer grandeur of the seated man (and the sense of embroilment produced by the red background) and the sitter's disappointingly benign face. Strong feelings appear to have been airbrushed out. The painting isn't in the same league as the drawings.

Købke made other "monumental" portraits at the time. ("Monumental" is the word most often used in relation to the painter's new, expanded aims.) The portraits were as much an effort to spread his wings as were the views of the north gate of the Citadel or the street scene in morning light; and like these large works, the portraits can call forth an ambivalent response. Købke's subjects included the artist Constantin Hansen, his sister Cecilie Margrethe Petersen, his friend Georg Hilker, and Jens Andreas Graah, a prefect. Taken as presentations of individuals, these pictures are alive. We believe that Købke caught the characters of his people precisely. And it somehow follows that, for an artist who apparently set so much store by what his teachers said, and whose father was so big a figure in his life, Købke's subjects for most of his large portraits are men.

The most spectacular piece of psychological analysis may be his paintings of Graah. A full-length portrait was commissioned by this Jutland magistrate, and along the way Købke made a half-length study (pl. 59) and many elegant drawings. Graah's portrait sends out a good whiff of a distinct person; we think we know the man, and he's distinctly unappealing. He's a little frightening. His controlling eyes and pursed mouth, taken with the bright red chamberlain's outfit that he wears, spell out a vain, imperious, condescending monster. (The man's face in many of the drawings is likable and sweet, because Købke used a young model for much of the work.) One reads about Graah with great relief. He turns out to have been everything Købke suggests, maybe worse. He was thought power-mad, meddlesome, and incompetent everywhere he served. An example of his bullying ways is the fact that, provincial prefect that he was, he would never have worn his honorary chamberlain's uniform to his office—and this portrait was commissioned for his office.

A string of qualities could be attributed to Købke's large portraits. No other Danish painter of the era was even thinking about the same note of directness and grandeur. And going from the spring-like image of Sødring to the brooding Freund and the haughty Graah, we see an artist who has grown in (or at least altered) his sense of people and the world. But we're not lured into thinking about how he made these pictures. There is little that is unique to Købke about the way they're painted; ultimately, they're a bit anonymous.

LAKE SORTEDAM

Even as Købke tried to master the big, public picture, he continued to make his own sort of intimate view painting—smaller pictures of a more informal nature. And a number of works finished between 1836 and 1838 show that these pictures, where less was at stake, were quietly taking on a new breadth. In many ways they're the real fruit of Købke's efforts to transform his art.

One of the first is a view across a field on a bright summer's day, toward a little settlement of houses by the water, with Copenhagen harbor and sailing ships in the far distance. *A View in the Neighborhood of the Lime Kiln, Looking Toward Copenhagen* (pl. 55), of 1836, is often singled out by Danes—and for good reason. At first sight, it's one more drowsy nineteenth-century pastoral; our eyes fall on a cow resting in the field, the sun glinting off her back. On a second viewing, Købke's exquisite sense of placement, proportion, and color becomes evident, and we can believe that this scene, where a tanned white makes up the top four-fifths (the sky), and a yellowed green makes up the bottom fifth (the field), is among his finest works. It's hard to say which is more masterful: Købke's weave of countless closely related greens and earth tones or the beautifully unemphatic way he has made the houses and trees the centerpiece of the picture—the centerpiece of the horizon line and the centerpiece as our eyes go from the picture's foreground back into its deep space.

The following year Købke made another view painting that, while not especially large, has the presence of a major work. The painter and his family had now been living by Lake Sortedam for more than three years. For his mother, as a souvenir, he went back to the Citadel to paint the northern drawbridge (pl. 56). The result, in the fully worked-out version, now in the National Gallery, London, may be the single most glorious demonstration of Købke's individuality as a colorist and designer. The bridge, the picture's main attraction, is painted "Købke red," yet with light coming up from the moat, the red has a glowing orange underside. But many elements in the picture contribute to an atmosphere, which we wouldn't associate with Købke, of carnival-like gaiety. There's a pink sky; a yellow house; pale, pale green saplings;

and an extraordinary sense of see-throughness. The picture almost seems to be about looking through things. We very much look through the waving grasses in the foreground to the scene itself, and then through the drawbridge to a stand of trees; and even the trees come in ranks, for behind the row of saplings is a row of older trees.

Impressive as the bay and the drawbridge paintings are, they can seem like preparations for three pictures dating from the next year, 1838. One is of two women on a dock, with the Danish flag fluttering in a light wind. Another is a view of a man walking along a path by the side of a lake, while the third shows a little party of people in various stages of ending an afternoon's boat ride. The three paintings have never been thought of as a unit, but, all set at Lake Sortedam and roughly the same size, they're variations on a theme. They're all about leave-taking. Each slightly different from the others in overall tone and each a complement to the others, they call out to be seen together in a single space. (They're actually in three different museums.) Two of them seem to be set at the exact same dock.

Christen Købke, *View from the Embankment of Lake Sortedam, Looking Toward Nørrebro*, 1838. Oil on canvas, 20⅞ × 28⅛″ (53 × 71.5 cm). Statens Museum for Kunst, Copenhagen.

The lakeside pictures are hardly "monumental" in size. They're on average fifteen inches high and twenty inches across. They're much smaller than *North Gate* and *Østerbro in Morning Light* and the larger views of Frederiksborg. Yet in what we sense were Købke's intentions, they, like the bay and drawbridge pictures, are enormous compared with his first successful view paintings—the scenes set along the Citadel ramparts. The Lake Sortedam pictures have the breathing room, the uncrowdedness, of big paintings.

These three works are of a piece with the early Citadel paintings, though, and they engage us in ways the Frederiksborg scenes and

Købke's other large paintings do not, in that the figures in them are more than pieces of local color. The figures—we barely see their faces—might be called the spirit of the respective scenes. Like Købke's earlier Citadel works, the lakeside pictures recall family snapshots; we automatically feel a connection between the artist and what he's showing us. These are genuine syntheses of his tight earlier works and his later attempts at a big style.

Presenting odd, and quite specific, hours and times and a dimming light, the Lake Sortedam paintings are about moments of perishable beauty. It's as if Købke had grown into the melancholy awareness that he had touched on a few years earlier, in the portraits of Christian Petersen and Lauritz Lyngbye. It's possible to look forward from these lakeside views, too—to say that the sense of emptiness and loss that seems to mark the painter's last ten years was foretold in them.

View from the Embankment of Lake Sortedam, Looking Toward Nørrebro (pl. 67), which shows two women on a dock, looking at a boat full

Christen Købke, *Autumn Morning at Lake Sortedam*, 1838. Oil on canvas, 13 × 18⅛" (33 × 46 cm). Ny Carlsberg Glyptotek, Copenhagen.

of people, is probably Købke's best-known work outside Denmark (from being reproduced in textbooks). Part of its beauty is that while the overall light is soft, almost gauzy, the light and shade in the clothing the women wear, and in the planks of the wood dock, are delineated with great precision. Købke so defines these and other details that the areas seem to emerge, like crust, from the surface. The effect recalls the way Watteau paints clothes (in his *fêtes galantes*). And Købke's moment of Copenhagen life—are the women waiting for the boat, or seeing it off?—shares the tense and ineffable drama of Watteau's art.

Lake Sortedam is portrayed in the fall in the picture of a man walking along a path called Lover's Lane (pl. 66). The time is early morning, perhaps on a November day, when the sunlight comes through the clouds as a plum purple-red. The stark, leafless trees and the man in the black overcoat and top hat, a sack of gloom gliding toward us, suggest Caspar David Friedrich's stage set–like mortality scenes. But Købke's subject is more the way the red light of the particular moment, in this particular time of year, filters through the wet, misty ivory-colored atmosphere and soaks up everything in the distance. Air, light, and color appear to be re-aligning themselves as we look. In an instant everything will be different.

It would be hard to say whether one Lake Sor-tedam painting is finer than the others. But the picture of the end of an afternoon's sail may be, as an image, the most resonant. *View from the Embankment of Lake Sortedam, Looking Toward Østerbro* (pl. 68), which shows some women starting to leave the pier, a child playing, and two men tidying up a boat, belongs to the Museum Stiftung Oskar Reinhart, in Winterthur, not far

Christen Købke, *View from the Embankment of Lake Sortedam, Looking Toward Østerbro*, 1838. Oil on canvas, 15½ × 19⅝″ (39.5 × 50 cm). Museum Stiftung Oskar Reinhart, Winterthur, Switzerland.

from Zurich. There it hangs in a room that presents the essence of what might be called Neoclassical, or Biedermeier, Realism. Besides Købke, two of the most individual painters associated with the era are represented here at their best. There are many works by Friedrich, in-cluding *Chalk Cliffs on Rügen*, perhaps his signature painting, and a small number by Wilhelm von Kobell, whose sunny scenes of people meeting on the roads outside Munich, with the Alps in the back-ground, are surprisingly tough studies in formal design. Although works by Købke now hang in the National Gallery in London, in the National Gallery of Scotland, and elsewhere, the painter's full mea-sure can best be taken at Winterthur, because there he holds forth in a conversation with two masters of his era. They are all presenting

Wilhelm von Kobell, *Riders by Tegernsee II*, 1825. Oil on panel, 13⅝ × 10¼" (34.5 × 26 cm). Museum Stiftung Oskar Reinhart, Winterthur, Switzerland.

Caspar David Friedrich, *Chalk Cliffs on Rügen*, 1818–19. Oil on canvas, 35⅜ × 27½" (90 × 70 cm). Museum Stiftung Oskar Reinhart, Winterthur, Switzerland.

the same subject, the leisure time of well-to-do but not noble people. All three painters show what might be called the Biedermeier afternoon.

Købke's Lake Sortedam painting and Friedrich's *Chalk Cliffs on Rügen* seem to have the most to say to each other, perhaps because they're both partly about water. Friedrich's painting shows a walking party, a woman in a red dress and two men, sitting or standing in a shady spot, looking out to an enveloping, arctic-bright amphitheater formed by the cliffs on this Baltic island. The picture seems to be about contemplation itself. We're hovering right along with this walking party; we share in their sense of serenity, infinitude, and the future. With Købke, we're more aware of being at a specific distance from the scene—we're watchers and listeners. His picture, with its subtly warmed light, is about the end of an activity. Water laps at the boat, which gently clonks against the pilings; feet are heard on the dock. Købke presents the moment when shadows start to cover the ground and evening is first felt in an afternoon.

Købke's chief image in the painting, and what a viewer probably remembers most, is the frieze-like row of people. They recall figures on a Greek vase and some of Seurat's Sunday-afternoon strollers. The best part of the frieze may be the two men bending down at the right end. The relation of their angular bodies leaning toward the mast, wonderfully capped by the top hat one of them wears, is the centerpiece of the work. The man in the top hat alone gives the painting the character of being a scene from a dream.

ITALY AND THE LONG LAST DECADE

Although Købke's art declined after 1838, the point has been made that his faculties, his sheer talent, were fully in place when he went south. The drawings he did in Italy, for instance, are the work of a formidable talent, ready to train his considerable technical abilities onto virtually anything his eyes alighted on. If Købke had turned into paintings his first drawings, from Rome and Venice—they show church interiors (pl. 69), squares, and arcades, with details of equal interest in every part of the square compositions—he might have made the most original works about Italy of any Danish artist. His large later drawings of architectural ruins (pl. 71) and beaches in Rome, Naples, Pompeii, and Capri, where seemingly every pebble, every crack in a toppled temple column, or every leaf on a twisting vine is delineated, are perhaps more accomplished than any drawings he had done in Denmark. But an academicism has set in. Coldly proficient techniques have taken over. The result isn't far from a steel engraving.

The painter went to Italy accompanied by his friend Georg Hilker, and without Sanne. The stipend for the trip, from the Academy, was just enough for the artists themselves; few of them traveled with their families. It has been suggested that during his stay, which lasted some two years, Købke was still on his anti-Eckersberg roll—still trying to shuck his first teacher. Where students of Mr. E., once in Italy, would trace the professor's steps, making their own versions of the small paintings he had made in Rome as a student, Købke, it is noted, didn't think of Rome as a place to work. His sights, perhaps set by Freund, were Naples and Pompeii. He also wanted to go to Capri, where the Blue Grotto had been discovered not many years before by German art students. And what attracted him in Capri were beaches and, especially, soaring cliffs, isolated against the sky—images of lordly grandeur that show how much Købke, at least in his choice of motifs, continued to be on the path of the immodest.

To judge from his letters, Købke loved his time in Italy. (While Rome wasn't his true destination, he managed to spend many months there, too.) And the small finished pictures and oil sketches he did in Italy—of the Castel dell'Uovo in Naples; of the forum at Pompeii (pl. 72); of various cliffs and coves in Capri (pl. 70)—are pleasant. (Not bearing the mark of a particular style, they hardly call out in a room.) Some have a soft, porous, light-filled appearance. In others, every crenellation of a cliff, every pebble on a beach, seems defined by sunlight. Købke also made oil copies after Pompeiian decorations and studies of waves breaking on a rocky shore.

In September 1840, having spent much of the previous two years in the company of fellow Danes, the painter returned to Copenhagen. He came home with plans for some ten large paintings based on his Italian shoreline themes. He appears to have thought that his impressions would now be the foundation of his major, public work. But his heart wasn't in it. Købke didn't paint at all during the first year back, and his output in general in the forties was erratic and sluggish. In the early part of the decade he started in on the Italian pictures, but he doesn't seem to have followed through on all of them. The concept must have become a millstone. He proposed a Capri shore scene to the Academy as his membership piece in 1842, with the idea that the picture, according to house rules, would be ready for viewing in two years. But in 1844 he needed an extension, which was for two years, and when he presented the painting in 1846—no one has ever thought it inspired—it was rejected.

Købke continued to make small pictures of the Lake Sortedam area and "cloud studies" (although he never exhibited them). These works have been compared with Constable and the French Impressionists, and many convey a sense of the painter himself standing in wind-blown, actual weather. All the leaves are rustling, everything is atwitter (as is true of many of his landscapes from the middle thirties on). There's also a hint of a new style in Købke's blocky, runny, halting way of putting down oil, first seen in sketches of crashing surf that he brought back from Italy. The blotchy complexion and wobbly yet rather elegant line of these works look forward to Fairfield Porter.

Yet most of Købke's lakeside scenes of the 1840s blend together. None compares with the three major paintings of 1838. The later works could stand some vigorous or sharp color. Købke seems to want only to capture a carefully modulated blond-and-brown tonality and a wet atmosphere. The pictures might present the state of someone who is mildly ravaged.

Købke also made pictures of his son and baby daughter and of mothers and children in his last years. It's logical that images of children and family life would have attracted him; but the faces in these pictures are literally blurry, and the mood is of a cottony, crestfallen sweetness. An admirer of the portraits of Fru Høyen or Christian Holm or Ida Thiele can find them hard to look at.

In addition to (or behind) Købke's inertia and his difficulty with new images, there were personal problems. In 1839, while he was in Italy, his brother Hans died; the next year Freund, only in his mid-fifties, and another brother, Carl, a pastor, died. Later Sanne was seriously ill for some time. Then, in 1843, Købke's father died. Two years later the big house on the Blegdam was sold, and Købke, Sanne, and their children moved to a considerably smaller house within the city. The next year, the Academy rejected his second membership bid. The rejection itself wasn't a catastrophe. Regardless of the quality of his picture, Købke wasn't the only painter who, for whatever reason, needed a number of tries to get into the Academy (Constantin Hansen received this uncertain distinction only decades later). But arriving on top of his family losses, and for an artist who was enjoying little sense of freedom or spontaneity in his work, the rejection was a blow.

Beset by money problems for the first time, Købke wrote in a letter that he believed he would ultimately be a painter of decorations. Did he think such a shift was a compromise? Two of his closest friends,

Freund and Hilker, had been seriously concerned with decoration in the antique world. And many other Danish artists of the era (and of eras before and after) were involved with various decorative schemes, including furniture design. There seems to be something in the very atmosphere that seduces the Scandinavian artist into making settings, or objects, that are less about the individual ego than about pleasing many people with unostentatiously comfortable and harmonious environments.

Købke actually did some decorative work in the 1840s. Like numerous other painters he had a hand in making ceiling frescoes—copies after antique paintings—for the new Thorvaldsen Museum. He also took some private commissions for work around Copenhagen. His designs for the walls for a local businessman's new stables survive. And in his parents' dining room he had already proved himself, presumably, a first-rate decorative artist.

Yet there was clearly a note of defeat in Købke's announcement. In his letters he says his desire is part of a dropping of goals, a lessening of challenges; he wants to have his decision represent a necessary curtailing of pride. He must also have believed that he had failed as a painter, at least momentarily. It's psychologically comprehensible, too, that Købke, who for most of his life hadn't supported himself with his art, might entertain the idea of becoming, in a professional sense, faceless—an anonymous designer.

A number of writers believe that Købke regained some of his earlier strength in the work he did in the year or so before he died. But his last really gripping image is a picture from 1845, of the garden gate to the Blegdam property (pl. 76). He is believed to have completed it (along with some others) after the family house had been sold that year. It might have been meant as a souvenir, and it does have the weight of a last glimpse of something. It appears to be Købke's only picture to show how people with houses on the Blegdam saw Lake Sortedam.

DENMARK

"It is a sad thing about small nationalities," wrote Graham Greene (about the Scots), "that like a possessive woman they trap their great men. . . . All have to some extent been made over by their countrymen, they have not been allowed to grow or to diminish with time." This is true—and yet not altogether true—of Købke. He has been written about for some time as the greatest talent in Danish painting, certainly of his own era, and some of his pictures represent for Danes what pictures by Winslow Homer represent for Americans: images of the nation at a bright and confident moment that manage not to be sentimental. The Golden Age of Danish painting is sometimes even referred to as the "Age of Købke." And I have heard some Danes reply when asked about him, "Oh yes, Købke—he is a hero to us."

Yet the accounts of the painter over the years strike one as almost weirdly well balanced. The writing about Købke the artist and the person is notable for its fair-mindedness, level-headedness, and wit. Marvelous as his biography is, Emil Hannover makes the barest references in it to Købke's contemporaries in the rest of Europe, let alone past masters. Even as Leo Swane, in a 1948 picture book on him, basically admires Købke, he treats him with a fairly powerful critical honesty, as when he says that Købke's "landscape art seems to belong in a distant little province which lived its own isolated life." There was no one, we read, "who had given him courage for a true painter's release." And while Købke's pictures and his life are treated with great sensitivity in recent works by Monrad and Norregård-Nielsen—writers with quite different approaches—he comes across (to American ears, at least) as less a powerful individual than a talented and hardworking figure of another time. None of the claims that American, English, French, German, or Italian writers routinely make about their own artists are made by any Dane about Købke.

Danish criticism and scholarly writing are, of course—it may take a little time to realize—in tune with the nature and emotion of Købke's work. On some level, the painter, who seems to have found the idea of a career in art somewhat paralyzing, probably would approve of the tone. He might approve of the way the decorative scheme for his parents' dining room, for example, remains about as private an affair now as it was in its day. Perhaps Købke would also comprehend how the Lake Sortedam pictures of 1838 have been admired individually but not celebrated as a group or as a culmination.

What a non-Danish viewer can feel, though, is how many aspects there are to Købke's art and how many styles and movements he adds to. He has been written about as a Biedermeier artist, and if one considers that most of his portraits are of family members and friends, and that the majority of his views are of places he lived in or near—and that none of these people or scenes is criticized or mocked in any way—he fits the term in the most obvious way. Yet Købke also vindicates the Biedermeier spirit. He puts a Spartan leanness on the taste for domesticity that characterizes the era.

By nature, Købke was a classical, a formal, artist. The Neoclassical style in one vein or another was an underpinning for many of the artists of Købke's day, including the realistic observers of the Biedermeier world. But Købke, in much the same spirit as the slightly earlier George Stubbs, made the idea of a ruled, measured sense of beauty a breathing part of himself. He clothed ideal proportions so fully in the garments and appearances of his time that at first we don't notice they are there.

Yet there was also a Romantic, or what we'd like to think was a Romantic, in Købke. There is no Romantic fever to his art (and in historical terms he wasn't a member of what might be called the first Romantic generation). Yet along with many of the artists, writers, and composers who were born, or were children, during the years between the French Revolution and Waterloo, Købke had something he ardently wanted to say when he was unusually young. Along with Kleist, Lermontov, Büchner, Runge, Palmer, Keats, Cotman, and others of the period (and along with many, of course, who didn't happen to make their work in extreme youth), he brought a more colloquial and personal intensity to his art.

It's hard to recall other paintings of the Romantic period, except Géricault's images of soldiers in moments of doubt and confusion, that convey so freshly the Romantic ache, the mixture of contrary yearnings, as Købke's *The Landscape Painter L. Lyngbye* (pl. 29). Troubled and leaning forward, Lyngbye might be seen as the hero of a Romantic work at a climactic moment. His face is remarkable, perhaps even in the company of the masterworks of European art, for the complex range of emotion it conveys. We can almost believe that Købke's ability to catch new degrees of light in the air led him to find new degrees of feeling in a face.

If the portrait of Frederik Sødring, with its sunny confidence, makes us stop and ask, "Who was Christen Købke?" the portrait of Lyngbye may be the picture that makes us believe we're seeing the painter's particular understanding of light and space, and people, taken to its extreme, its limit. The portraits hardly sum up his achievement. The sparkling small early views of life along the Citadel ramparts, where Købke's sense of design is at its most brilliant and unpredictable, may be fresher now than the day they were made. And it's in his pictures for the house on Blegdamsvej, and then in the Lake Sortedam paintings, that he made a seamless whole of his feelings for the beauty of the natural world and for the note of uncertainty beneath it.

In the portraits of Sødring and Lyngbye, Købke might be presenting, rather, certain poles, or foundations, of his temperament. He also seems to encompass two of the foundations of Danish life and thought of the time. Looking at one portrait and then the other, we can understand how that time produced both Andersen, with his novel appreciation of life's minutiae, and Kierkegaard, who made a kind of poetry out of the difficulty of belief. We can understand why Danish art historians, even as they describe his achievement with the lightest hand, still call his era the "Age of Købke."

PLATES

PLATE I
Marstrand at the Easel in Eckersberg's Studio, 1829. Oil on canvas, 11 ¼ × 8 ⅝" (28.5 × 22 cm). Nationalhistoriske Museum på Frederiksborg, Hillerød.

PLATE 2
*The Painter C. D. Gebauer Drawing Miss
Margrethe Holm*, 1829. Pencil, 6 ½ × 8 ½″
(16.4 × 21.5 cm). Kongelige
Kobberstiksamling, Statens Museum for
Kunst, Copenhagen.

PLATE 3
Portrait of Fru W. Høegh-Guldberg, 1829.
Oil on canvas, 9⅛ × 7⅞″ (23.1 × 19.9 cm).
Kunstmuseum, Aarhus.

PLATE 4
*View of the Square in the Citadel, Looking
Toward the Embankment*, 1830. Oil on
canvas, 11¾ × 9¼″ (30 × 23.5 cm).
National Gallery of Scotland, Edinburgh.

PLATE 5
*The Cigar Seller by the Northern Gate of the
Citadel*, 1830. Oil on canvas, 9 × 9⅞″
(23 × 25 cm). Private collection,
Denmark.

PLATE 6
A View from a Storehouse in the Citadel,
1831. Oil on canvas, 15 ⅜ × 12″ (39 × 30.5
cm). Statens Museum for Kunst,
Copenhagen.

PLATE 7
Ida Thiele, 1832. Oil on canvas, 8⅞ × 7⅞"
(22.5 × 20 cm). Statens Museum for Kunst,
Copenhagen.

PLATE 8
Inger Margrethe Høyen, 1832. Oil on
canvas, 12 × 9⅞″ (30.5 × 25 cm). Statens
Museum for Kunst, Copenhagen.

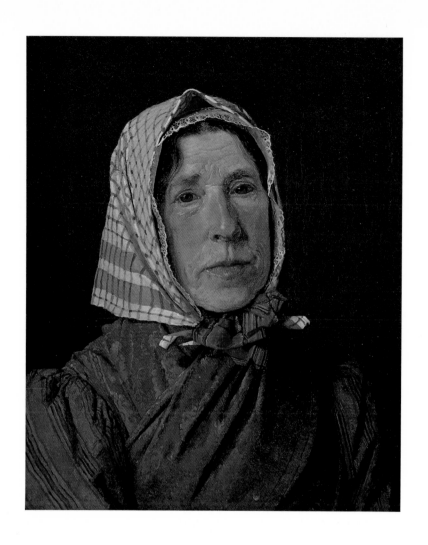

PLATE 9
An Old Farmer Woman, 1832. Oil on
canvas, 12¼ × 9⅞″ (31 × 25 cm).
Kunstmuseum, Randers.

PLATE 10
An Old Sailor, 1832. Oil on canvas,
12¼ × 10⅝″ (31 × 27 cm). Statens Museum
for Kunst, Copenhagen.

PLATE 11 (*left*)
Young Man Sitting on a Sofa Reading.
Pencil, 6 ½ × 4 ⅛" (16.4 × 10.5 cm).
Kongelige Kobberstiksamling, Statens
Museum for Kunst, Copenhagen.

PLATE 12 (*right*)
Study for the Portrait of Conradine Feilberg,
1832. Oil on canvas, 12 ¼ × 8 ¼" (31 × 21
cm). Private collection, Denmark.

PLATE 13
Adolphine Petersen, 1832. Oil on canvas,
11¾ × 9⅞″ (30 × 25 cm). Private collection,
Denmark.

PLATE 14
Eckersberg and Marstrand on a Study
Excursion, 1832. Pencil, 5¾ × 7¼″
(14.7 × 18.4 cm). Kongelige
Kobberstiksamling, Statens Museum for
Kunst, Copenhagen.

PLATE 15
The Landscape Painter F. Sødring, 1832. Oil
on canvas, 16⅝ × 14⅞″ (42.2 × 37.8 cm).
Hirschsprungske Samling, Copenhagen.

PLATE 16
View from a Window on Toldbodvej. Pencil
and sepia, 8 ⅝ × 7 ⅛″ (21.8 × 18 cm).
Kongelige Kobberstiksamling, Statens
Museum for Kunst, Copenhagen.

PLATE 17
View of the Courtyard of the Citadel's Bakery,
1832. Oil on canvas, 13 × 9½″ (33 × 24 cm).
Ny Carlsberg Glyptotek, Copenhagen.

PLATE 18
Christian Petersen, 1833. Oil on canvas,
12⅜ × 10⅝″ (31.5 × 27 cm). Statens
Museum for Kunst, Copenhagen.

PLATE 19
*View of the Citadel from a Window on
Toldbodvej*, 1833. Oil on paper mounted on
canvas, 5⅞ × 10⅞″ (15 × 27.5 cm). Statens
Museum for Kunst, Copenhagen.

PLATE 20
Classen's Garden Outside Copenhagen, 1833.
Oil on paper; 5 ⅞ × 9 ¼″ (15 × 23.5 cm).
Statens Museum for Kunst, Copenhagen.

PLATE 21
The Painter and Lithographer P. H.
Gemzøe, 1833. Oil on canvas, 22⅝ × 18⅞″
(57.5 × 48 cm). Statens Museum for Kunst,
Copenhagen.

PLATE 22
Male Model, 1833. Oil on canvas,
21¼ × 17⅜″ (54 × 44 cm).
Kunstakademiet, Copenhagen.

PLATE 23
Professor F. C. Sibbern, 1833. Pencil and
sepia, 9¾ × 7⅛″ (24.7 × 18.7 cm).
Kongelige Kobberstiksamling, Statens
Museum for Kunst, Copenhagen.

PLATE 24
Portrait of B. Høyen, 1833. Oil on canvas,
8¼×6⅞″ (21×17.6 cm). Hirschsprungske
Samling, Copenhagen.

*View from the Citadel Wall, with the Towers
of the Church of Our Lady and St. Petri
Church in the Background,* 1833. Oil on
paper, mounted on canvas, 6 ¼ × 11 ⅝″
(16 × 29.5 cm). Hirschsprungske Samling,
Copenhagen.

PLATE 27 (top)
Frederiksborg Castle, 1833. Pencil,
6⅝ × 11⅛″ (16.9 × 28.3 cm).
Hirschsprungske Samling, Copenhagen.

PLATE 28 (bottom)
The Frederiksborg Castle Courtyard. India
ink, 9⅝ × 6¼″ (24.3 × 16 cm). Kongelige
Kobberstiksamling, Statens Museum for
Kunst, Copenhagen.

PLATE 29
The Landscape Painter L. Lyngbye, 1833. Oil
on canvas, 10½ × 8½″ (26.6 × 21.5 cm).
Hirschsprungske Samling, Copenhagen.

PLATE 30 *(top)*
*View from the Citadel Embankment Looking
Toward the Battery "Trekroner,"* 1833. Oil
on canvas, 7 ⅝ × 11 ⅜″ (19.5 × 29 cm).
Statens Museum for Kunst, Copenhagen.

PLATE 31 *(bottom)*
View from Langelinie. Pencil, 6 ½ × 10″
(16.5 × 25.3 cm). Kongelige
Kobberstiksamling, Statens Museum for
Kunst, Copenhagen.

PLATE 32
*View of Langelinie and the Sound from the
Citadel Embankment*, 1833. Oil on canvas,
9½ × 13″ (24 × 33 cm). Hirschsprungske
Samling, Copenhagen.

PLATE 33
*Portion of the North Gate of the Citadel Seen
from the Bastion East of the Bridge*, 1833–34.
Oil on canvas, 9¼ × 12⅝" (23.6 × 32 cm).
Hirschsprungske Samling, Copenhagen.

PLATE 34
One of the Turrets at Frederiksborg Castle,
1834. Oil on canvas, 10 × 7 ¼″ (25.5 × 18.5
cm). Davids Samling, Copenhagen.

PLATE 35
Sailors (or *Studies for "View Outside the North Gate of the Citadel"*). Pencil, 10 ½ × 8 ⅛″ (26.6 × 20.8 cm). Kongelige Kobberstiksamling, Statens Museum for Kunst, Copenhagen.

PLATE 36
View Outside the North Gate of the Citadel,
1834. Oil on canvas, 31⅛ × 36⅝″ (79 × 93
cm). Ny Carlsberg Glyptotek,
Copenhagen.

PLATE 37
Johanne Pløyen, 1834. Oil on canvas,
9⅞ × 7⅝″ (25 × 19.5 cm). Statens Museum
for Kunst, Copenhagen.

PLATE 38
The Animal Painter Christian Holm, 1834.
Oil on canvas, 10 ¼ × 8 ⅛″ (26 × 20.5 cm).
Statens Museum for Kunst, Copenhagen.

PLATE 39
*The Roof of Frederiksborg Castle, with a
View Toward Lake, Town, and Woods.*
Pencil and India ink, 8 ¼ × 7 ¼" (21 × 18.3
cm). Kongelige Kobberstiksamling,
Statens Museum for Kunst, Copenhagen.

PLATE 40
*Portrait of a Naval Officer, D. Christen
Schifter Feilberg*, 1834. Oil on canvas,
20⅝ × 14¼″ (52.5 × 37.5 cm). Statens
Museum for Kunst, Copenhagen.

PLATE 41
Night (after Thorvaldsen's relief), 1834–35.
Oil on canvas, 29⅞ × 29⅞″ (76 × 76 cm).
Davids Samling, Copenhagen.

PLATE 42
Day (after Thorvaldsen's relief), 1834–35.
Oil on canvas, 29⅞ × 29⅞″ (76 × 76 cm).
Davids Samling, Copenhagen.

PLATE 43
One of the Turrets at Frederiksborg Castle,
1834–35. Oil on canvas, 69⅝ × 63¾″
(177 × 162 cm). Danske
Kunstindustrimuseum, Copenhagen.

PLATE 44
The Roof of Frederiksborg Castle, with a
View Toward Lake, Town, and Woods,
1834–35. Oil on canvas, 69⅝ × 67⅜″
(177 × 171 cm). Danske
Kunstindustrimuseum, Copenhagen.

PLATE 45
*Frederiksborg Castle in Evening Light
(study)*, 1835. Oil on paper, mounted on
board, 8¾ × 13⅛″ (22.2 × 33.5 cm).
Hirschsprungske Samling, Copenhagen.

PLATE 46
Peter Købke, the Artist's Father, 1835. Oil
on canvas, 9 ¼ × 7 ⅞" (23.5 × 20 cm).
Statens Museum for Kunst, Copenhagen.

PLATE 47
*Cecilie Margrethe Købke, the Artist's
Mother*, 1835. Oil on canvas, 9¼ × 7⅞"
(23.5 × 20 cm). Statens Museum for Kunst,
Copenhagen.

PLATE 48
Studies for the Painting "Frederiksborg
Castle Seen from the Northwest," 1836.
Pencil, 11½ × 8½″ (29.3 × 21.6 cm).
Kongelige Kobberstiksamling, Statens
Museum for Kunst, Copenhagen.

PLATE 49
*Frederiksborg Castle Seen from the
Northwest (study)*, 1835. Oil on paper,
mounted on canvas, 9½ × 10⅝″ (24 × 27
cm). Statens Museum for Kunst,
Copenhagen.

PLATE 50 *(top)*
*The Street with the Water Pump (Study for
"Østerbro in Morning Light")*, 1836.
Pencil, 5⅞ × 8⅜″ (14.8 × 21.3 cm).
Kongelige Kobberstiksamling, Statens
Museum for Kunst, Copenhagen.

PLATE 51 *(bottom)*
Cows, 1836. Pencil, 4 × 6¾″ (10.2 × 17.2
cm). Kunstmuseum, Aarhus.

PLATE 52
Østerbro in Morning Light, 1836. Oil on
canvas, 41⅞ × 63⅝" (106.5 × 161.5 cm).
Statens Museum for Kunst, Copenhagen.

PLATE 53
Frederiksborg Castle Seen from the
Northwest, 1836. Oil on canvas,
22 7/8 × 25 1/4″ (58 × 64 cm). Statens Museum
for Kunst, Copenhagen.

PLATE 54
Wilhelm Marstrand, 1836. Oil on canvas,
7 ¼ × 5 ⅞″ (18.5 × 15 cm). Statens Museum
for Kunst, Copenhagen.

PLATE 55
A View in the Neighborhood of the Lime Kiln,
Looking Toward Copenhagen, 1836. Oil on
canvas, 14⅜ × 22⅝″ (36.5 × 57.5 cm).
Nivaagaards Malerisamling, Nivå.

PLATE 56
*View of the Northern Drawbridge to the
Citadel*, 1837. Oil on canvas, 17 ¾ × 25 ¾"
(45 × 65.5 cm). National Gallery, London.

PLATE 57 *(top)*
Autumn Landscape. Frederiksborg Castle in the Middle Distance, c. 1837. Oil on canvas, 10 × 14″ (25.5 × 35.5 cm). Ny Carlsberg Glyptotek, Copenhagen.

PLATE 58 *(bottom)*
Maren Krohn, 1837. Pencil, 6⅝ × 5¾″ (16.9 × 14.6 cm). Kongelige Kobberstiksamling, Statens Museum for Kunst, Copenhagen.

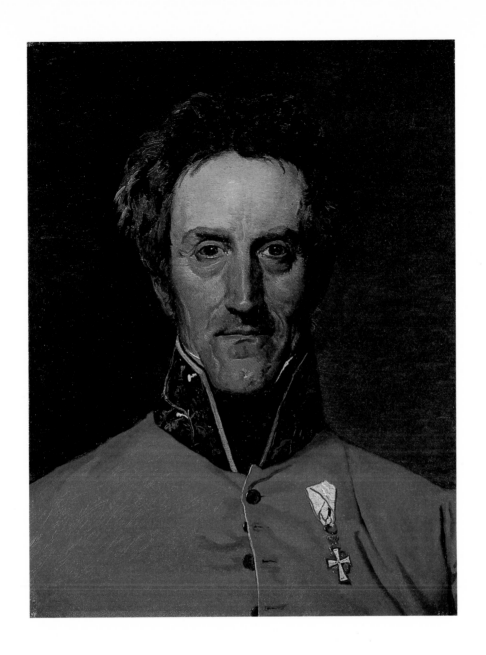

PLATE 59
Study for the Portrait of Prefect J. A. Graah,
1837–38. Oil on canvas, 19⅝ × 15⅛″
(50 × 38.5 cm). Ny Carlsberg Glyptotek,
Copenhagen.

PLATE 60
Valdemar Hjartvar Købke, the Artist's Brother, 1838. Oil on canvas, 21⅛ × 18¼″ (53.7 × 46.4 cm). The Metropolitan Museum of Art, New York, Purchase, 1990 (1990.233).

PLATE 61 *(left)*
The Artist's Brother, H. P. N. Købke. Pencil,
6¾ × 5⅜″ (17.1 × 13.8 cm). Kongelige
Kobberstiksamling, Statens Museum for
Kunst, Copenhagen.

PLATE 62 *(right)*
*Portrait of the Artist's Wife, Susanne Cecilie
Købke*, 1838. Pencil, 8⅝ × 6¾″ (22 × 17.2
cm). Kongelige Kobberstiksamling,
Statens Museum for Kunst, Copenhagen.

PLATE 63 (left)
Portrait of H. E. Freund, 1837. Pencil, with
white chalk on gray-beige chalk-treated
paper, 7 5/8 × 6 1/4″ (19.5 × 16 cm).
Hirschsprungske Samling, Copenhagen.

PLATE 64 (right)
Portrait of H. E. Freund, 1838. Pencil,
17 1/8 × 10 3/8″ (43.5 × 26.5 cm).
Hirschsprungske Samling, Copenhagen.

PLATE 65
The Sculptor Hermann Ernst Freund, 1838.
Oil on canvas, 62 ¼ × 37 ¾″ (158 × 96 cm).
Kunstakademiet, Copenhagen.

PLATE 66
Autumn Morning at Lake Sortedam, 1838.
Oil on canvas, 13 × 18 ⅛″ (33 × 46 cm). Ny
Carlsberg Glyptotek, Copenhagen.

PLATE 67
*View from the Embankment of Lake
Sortedam, Looking Toward Nørrebro*, 1838.
Oil on canvas, 20⅞ × 28⅛″ (53 × 71.5 cm).
Statens Museum for Kunst, Copenhagen.

PLATE 68
*View from the Embankment of Lake
Sortedam, Looking Toward Østerbro*, 1838.
Oil on canvas, 15 ½ × 19 ⅝″ (39.5 × 50 cm).
Museum Stiftung Oskar Reinhart,
Winterthur, Switzerland.

PLATE 69
Ss. Giovanni e Paolo, Venice, 1838. Pencil,
10⅛ × 7⅝″ (25.7 × 19.3 cm). Kongelige
Kobberstiksamling, Statens Museum for
Kunst, Copenhagen.

PLATE 70
Marina Grande, Capri, 1839–40. Oil on
paper, mounted on canvas, 15 ½ × 21 ¼"
(39.5 × 54 cm). Kunstmuseum, Aarhus.

PLATE 72
*The Forum: Pompeii, with Vesuvius in the
Distance*, 1841. Oil on canvas, 27 × 34″
(68.5 × 86.3 cm). The J. Paul Getty
Museum, Malibu, California.

PLATE 73 *(top)*
The Front Yard of Baker Køhke's House,
c. 1841–45. Pencil, 6⅝ × 9⅝″ (16.7 × 24.5
cm). Kongelige Kobberstiksamling,
Statens Museum for Kunst, Copenhagen.

PLATE 74 *(bottom)*
*The Artist's Brother-in-Law, Captain C. B.
Køhke*, 1841. Pencil, 8 × 6⅜″ (20.4 × 16.3
cm). Kongelige Kobberstiksamling,
Statens Museum for Kunst, Copenhagen.

PLATE 75
The Garden Stairs to the Artist's Studio at the Blegdam, c. 1841–45. Oil on paper, mounted on canvas, 8⅞ × 13″ (22.5 × 33 cm). Statens Museum for Kunst, Copenhagen.

PLATE 76
The Garden Gate at the Blegdam, c. 1841–
45. Oil on paper, mounted on canvas,
11⅝ × 9⅝″ (29.5 × 24.5 cm). Statens
Museum for Kunst, Copenhagen.

Christen Købke.
Efter en Pennetegning af P. C. Skovgaard.

Workshop of F. Hendriksen, after a
drawing by P. C. Skovgaard, *Portrait of
Christen Købke*. Woodcut, 6 ⅛ × 5 ⅝"
(15.7 × 14.2 cm). Kongelige
Kobberstiksamling, Statens Museum for
Kunst, Copenhagen.

CHRONOLOGY

1810   Christen Schiellerup Købke born May 26 in Copenhagen, one of eleven children, to Peter Berendt and Cecilie Margrethe Købke.

1817   Moves with his family to the Citadel, where his father runs the bakery.

1821   Begins drawing to give himself something to do during a long illness.

1822   Enters the Royal Academy of Fine Arts, at Charlottenborg Palace.

1828   After studying with Christian August Lorentzen, becomes a student at Charlottenborg of the painter Christoffer Wilhelm Eckersberg.

1829   Stays in Aarhus with friends during the summer; possibly has a love affair, and does some of the first pictures where his feeling for color and light is evident.

1831   Around the beginning of the year, in his debut, exhibits *The Cigar Seller by the Northern Gate of the Citadel*; *Portion of the Plaster Cast Collection at Charlottenborg*; and *View of the Square in the Citadel, Looking Toward the Embankment*, among others, and sells a few; rents a studio on Toldbodvej, not far from the Citadel; in the summer, in Hillerød, helps care for his sister Conradine Feilberg during a difficult period after the birth of her child; there gets to know the art historian, critic, and curator Niels Lauritz Høyen, who is assembling pictures for Frederiksborg Castle.

1832   No longer takes formal instruction at the Academy, but continues to study privately with Eckersberg.

1833   Moves with his family to the Blegdam by Lake Sortedam, just outside Copenhagen, at the end of the year.

1834   From July through October, paints *View Outside the North Gate of the Citadel*, his first commission and first truly public effort, which is ordered by the Kunstforening; begins making a decorative scheme, using images of Frederiksborg Castle and Bertel Thorvaldsen's sculpture, for the dining room of his family's new house.

1835   Works further on the dining room scheme and on paintings of Frederiksborg Castle seen at sunset from the northwest.

1836   Completes the large *Østerbro in Morning Light*; is engaged to Susanne Cecilie Købke (Sanne), a cousin, in the spring; by summer has begun to pay serious heed to the sculptor Hermann Ernst Freund, whose studio-home is open to younger painters, and to read more deeply in pietistic literature.

1837   Travels with Freund during the summer; is married to Susanne in November.

1838   Exhibits *Autumn Morning at Lake Sortedam* at Charlottenborg in April; in August leaves for Italy with decorative artist Georg Christian Hilker; visits Verona, Padua, and Venice before arriving in Rome shortly before Christmas.

1839   In the spring leaves Rome for Naples and farther south, where he had long planned to work; from September until around Christmas is in Capri, then back in Naples; at Charlottenborg, *View from the Embankment at Lake Sortedam, Looking Toward Nørrebro* and *View from the Embankment of Lake Sortedam, Looking Toward Østerbro* are exhibited.

1840   In the spring is back in Capri, then at Pompeii; at the end of July begins the trip home; in September is back in Copenhagen; Freund dies in August.

1841   First child, Hans Peter Carl, is born, with many complications and prolonged recovery for Sanne.

1842   Academy approves his proposal of a Capri subject as his membership piece, to be finished, according to Academy rules, within two years.

1843   Peter Købke, the painter's father, dies.

1844   Obtains an extension for two years on delivery of his painting for Academy membership; works with other artists in the new Thorvaldsen Museum in Copenhagen, painting ceiling decorations in a classical manner.

1845   Continues working in the Thorvaldsen Museum, and does commissioned decorative work for a stable; second child, Juliane Emilie, is born; family house at Blegdamsvej 15 is sold by spring; moves with his wife and children to a section of Copenhagen.

1846   In October, the Academy rejects his membership painting.

1848   Dies on February 7, not yet thirty-eight, of pneumonia; in mid-April an auction of his work is held in his studio.

1849   Sanne, seriously ill on and off throughout her marriage, dies.

Christen Købke, *The Painter Gemzøe
Drawing Outdoors*. Pencil, 8⅝ × 6½″
(21.8 × 16.5 cm). Kongelige
Kobberstiksamling, Statens Museum for
Kunst, Copenhagen.

The writing on Købke is primarily in Danish. Emil Hannover's ground-breaking biography, *Maleren Christen Købke*, was published in 1893. The second foundation for thinking about the artist is Mario Krohn's 1915 illustrated catalogue, *Maleren Christen Købkes Arbejder*, a compact volume that includes background information about many of the pictures and passages from Købke's letters.

Among the other Danish writers who have produced little picture books or essays on Købke over the years are Karl Madsen (who wrote an introduction to a book of Købke's drawings in 1929); Henrik Bramsen (1942); Jørn Rubow (1945); and Leo Swane (1948). Like Hannover, many of these men worked in museums and/or were painters themselves, and they have pointed and lively opinions about pictures.

Among specialized art historical essays about Købke are Arne Brenna's major study of the portrait of Hermann Ernst Freund, which appeared in the 1974 bulletin of the Statens Museum for Kunst, and Anne-Birgitte Fonsmark's study of the portrait of Jens Andreas Graah, which appeared in a 1981 Ny Carlsberg Glyptotek review supplement. In a 1983 Glyptotek bulletin, Fonsmark writes at length about Købke in Capri.

The two leading writers about Købke for the past decade are Kasper Monrad and Hans Edvard Nørregård-Nielsen. Monrad's 1984 *Danish Painting: The Golden Age*, which features introductory essays by Henrik Bramsen and Alistair Smith, and was published by the National Gallery, London, is out of print (and a rarity in London bookshops). Monrad is the author also of the finely detailed *Købke pa Blegdammen og ved Sortedamssøen*, a 1981 Statens Museum for Kunst catalogue on what might be called the Sortedam years, and of

Christen Købke, *Seated Dog, After an Antique Sculpture at Charlottenborg*, 1836. Etching, 3¾ × 3⅝″ (9.4 × 9.2 cm). Kongelige Kobberstiksamling, Statens Museum for Kunst, Copenhagen.

articles on other aspects of Købke's work. Monrad's *Hverdagsbilleder* (Pictures of Everyday Life), published in 1989, brings together representative pictures and a wealth of information on many aspects of all the painters of the time, with a particular emphasis on the artists as social beings: How much did they earn? What commissions came their way? (A précis in English can be found toward the back of the volume.)

Norregård-Nielsen, in contrast, sees Købke and his art as an entryway to a more literary and cultural overview of the Golden Age. He is the author of a small 1980 biography of Købke and a 1981 Glyptotek catalogue entitled *Købke og Kastellet*, about the Citadel period. Various Norregård-Nielsen radio talks on the painter have recently been brought together in *Undervejs med Christen Købke* (On the Road with Christen Købke). Like his Glyptotek catalogue, this is a novel-like work, full of lengthy quotations from Købke's letters. It should not be confused with Norregård-Nielsen's eventual biography of the painter.

Vagn Poulsen's *Danish Painting and Sculpture* was written to acquaint English-speaking people with the subject, and a second edition, revised by Norregård-Nielsen (1976), is available. Poulsen's presentation of centuries of Danish art has a wry, affectionate, and gentlemanly tone that belies many shrewd observations. Also available in English is *C. W. Eckersberg and His Pupils*, a collection of four articles that originally appeared in *C. W. Eckersberg og hans elever*, an illustrated 1984 catalogue published by the Statens Museum.

Beside Robert Rosenblum, Fritz Novotny, and Geraldine Norman, whose books are mentioned in the Introduction, Peter Galassi touches on Købke (and Eckersberg) in *Before Photography*, the catalogue of a 1981 Museum of Modern Art (New York) exhibition of the same name. Developing an idea put forth by Heinrich Schwarz, Galassi shows how the private, informal, sketch-like paintings of European artists in the early nineteenth century have many of the qualities associated with photographs. Did this sort of painting, with its feeling for an angled, partial, informal, and tense way of seeing, spur the invention of photography? There can't be an answer, but the paintings here form a stimulating portfolio.

Writings in English about literary and other aspects of the Danish Golden Age are not overwhelming in number. The figure of the time who has inspired the greatest amount of commentary is Søren Kierkegaard, whose own enormous body of work is available in English. Of the many essays and books about him, the most wide-ranging, penetrating, and pleasurable may be Josiah Thompson's *Kierkegaard* (1973). (Why it is out of print is a mystery.) Henning Fenger's *Kierkegaard: The Myths and Their Origins*, translated in 1980 from the Danish, is a witty reply to many Kierkegaard studies. Fenger touches on one down-to-earth element that Thompson, whose interest is philosophy, doesn't emphasize: Kierkegaard as a writer of Danish and as a writer in a certain moment of European literary history.

Along the way, Fenger brings a number of other literary figures of the Golden Age to life. He describes what might be Hans Christian Andersen's true claim to the fame he sought 'round the clock—that is, his introduction, in his stories and early novels, which are virtually unknown in the English-speaking world, of a racing, colloquial, modern Danish. Roger Sale, in *Fairy Tales and After* (1978), minces no words in presenting Andersen's limitations. Rumer Godden, in a 1966 biography, *Hans Christian Andersen*, sees his failings but writes, in a light, sketchy, and sunny style that might approximate Andersen's, as an admirer.

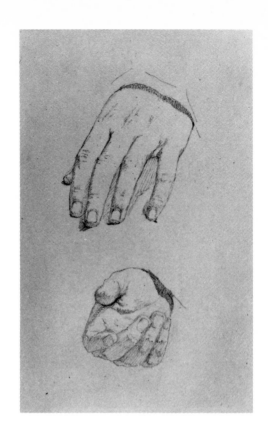

Christen Købke, *Studies of Hands*. Pencil,
6⅜ × 4″ (16.1 × 10.2 cm). Kongelige
Kobberstiksamling, Statens Museum for
Kunst, Copenhagen.

SEEING KØBKE'S PICTURES

As noted in the Introduction, a handful of pictures by Købke have entered museums in Great Britain and the United States, primarily in recent years. There is one Købke in France, a very modest sketch in the Louvre, and one in Switzerland: the masterwork in the Museum Stiftung Oskar Reinhart, in Winterthur. Surprisingly, there are no pictures by Købke in German museums. Scandinavian collections include a work in Oslo, one in Göteborg, and five fine if not transcendent paintings in Stockholm's National Museum.

Seeing Købke's work means going to his homeland, and most of his pictures are in museums in and around Copenhagen. The largest and most comprehensive collection by far, as the captions in this volume hint, is that of the Statens Museum for Kunst (referred to also as the Royal Museum of Fine Arts). The museum owns so many of Købke's paintings that there isn't space for all of them to be shown at once, but it is possible to arrange to see those that are in storage. It's easy to see Købke's drawings and prints there; no advance appointment is necessary to have the staff of the Kongelige Kobberstiksamling (also called the Department of Prints and Drawings) bring them out.

Copenhagen's other leading museum, the Ny Carlsberg Glyptotek, is known for its esteemed collection of classical and ancient art, and French nineteenth-century art. The Glyptotek also has a number of significant Danish paintings, including Købke's *View Outside the North Gate of the Citadel* and *Autumn Morning at Lake Sortedam*. If he somehow doesn't come across as

Christen Købke, *Peter Købke, Sophie Krohn, and N. Feilberg*, c. 1834. Lithograph, 6¾ × 10¾″ (17.2 × 27.2 cm). Kongelige Kobberstiksamling, Statens Museum for Kunst, Copenhagen.

powerfully here as at the Statens Museum, it's not simply because the latter collection is bigger. Købke the portraitist is not much in evidence at the Glyptotek, and that may be why these Købkes, even with *Autumn Morning* among them, don't add up to more than many different aspects of the artist.

Sharing a park with the Statens Museum for Kunst is the Hirschsprung Collection. Presenting, among other strong works, Købke's portraits of Lyngbye, Fru Høyen, and Sødring in a single room there (together with Bendz's Amalienborg interior), this museum is crucial for the viewer of Købke's art. A tobacco manufacturer, Heinrich Hirschsprung undersaw the creation of the impressive building—it is both massive and intimate—that houses his large collection of Danish pictures. The small paintings of the Golden Age are hung tooth by jowl, which may be how they were once hung, but which means that, on a first view, it takes some extra time to get one's bearings. The building overall, however, as a place to show art, is extraordinary. The light and the flow of the rooms make it an ideal setting for pictures of any size.

Købke's *Day* and *Night* paintings, along with the superb small version of the Frederiksborg turret, are in the David Collection, primarily a museum of decorative art. This collection includes a large Købke portrait of an older man and some sumptuous portrait drawings by Jens Juel. (The treasure of the collection is probably the handsomely displayed Islamic art, which is set in cabinet-like rooms in an upstairs annex that might be missed by the casual museumgoer).

The other half of the dining room scheme, the Frederiksborg rooftop paintings, are in the Danske Kunstindustrimuseum, another museum of decorative art. There are also two Købke portraits here, which actually belong to the Statens Museum; the sheer craftsmanship in *Fru Henriette Petersen* is enough to make this a work to search out. The Kunstindustrimuseum, whose collection of furniture and modern design pieces is extensive and beautifully displayed, is exceptional in itself. The building, a few blocks away from the royal palace, was constructed in the 1750s as a hospital (it is where Kierkegaard spent the last weeks of his life and where he died). It is in the shape of a square, in the center of which is a garden with benches and lime avenues—where the patients originally could take some air. There are windows on both sides of the building, but walking through the rooms, we're primarily aware of those on the inner, garden wall. The garden, with its trees, and the big sky are very much a part of the Kunstindustrimuseum.

The Ordrupgaard Collection, in Charlottenlund, a park-like suburb of Copenhagen, owns a number of Købke's paintings plus other Danish paintings (and a powerhouse collection of nineteenth-century French pictures, including Delacroix's portrait of George Sand and a room of Gauguins). The most impressive Købke in this elegant museum may be one of his small, postcard-like views from the Citadel earth mounds. The sun is felt everywhere in this painting, but it's seen bathing only a tiny patch of wall on a building at the far left.

Also outside of Copenhagen is the Nivaagaard Painting Collection. It is in Nivå, on the Sound, not far from Louisiana, the well-known museum of twentieth-century European and American art. The Nivaagaard Collection has only one Købke painting, the exquisite and serene *A View in the Neighborhood of the Lime Kiln, Looking Toward Copenhagen*. The other holdings may not be of the same order, but the newer part of the museum especially, which resembles a long, low shed that has sunk gently down into the grass, presents itself with an unassumingness that, to an American museumgoer, at least, is equally disarming and appealing.

There are works by Købke in museums in Odense (on the island of Funen), and in Aarhus, Ribe, and Randers (in Jutland), among others. A viewer in search of Købke's work might also visit Ramlose and Hillerød—less for the pictures than for the places themselves. Ramlose is a tiny village not far from the northern coast of Zealand. In the little white medieval church there is Købke's one religious work, a touching and interesting, but not really satisfying, picture of Christ as he appears to Nicodemus. The light on the hat and clothes of Nicodemus, who turns away from us, is dazzling; but there is no overall tension to this Rembrandt-like picture, perhaps because the Christ figure is characterless. Købke began work on the altarpiece after he became engaged, in 1836, and didn't finish it until sometime in 1838. It seems to have been a kind of soul mate for him during this time of groping, when he fell back on reserves of piety to sustain himself, even as he nosed around for new ideas.

Hillerød, the site of Frederiksborg Castle, is fairly close to Copenhagen. If you are going there by car, and for the first time, you might miss the proper turn that takes you past the buildings of Hillerød and to the castle. But the searching is part of the experience. Especially if you know Frederiksborg only through Købke's images, your first view of it, as it suddenly comes into view, placid and immense—rather like a sperm whale turning up one morning in the village harbor—can be heart-stopping. The building Købke painted in the 1830s was much destroyed by a fire in 1859. What we look at today is an exact reconstruction, done later in the nineteenth century. This fact doesn't get in the way of our involuntarily putting ourselves in Købke's mind, seeing the castle as he did, as we go around the place. The castle has for a long time been a national history museum—a national portrait gallery, really—so inside, beside Købke's very early portrait of Wilhelm Marstrand at an easel, one seems to encounter the entire nation.

Index